Speaking and Listening for All

Sylvia Edwards

David Fulton Publishers
London

David Fulton Publishers Ltd
Ormond House, 26-27 Boswell Street, London WC1N 3JD

First published in Great Britain by David Fulton Publishers 1999

British Library Cataloguing in Publication Data
A catalogue record for this book is available from the British Library

ISBN 1-85346-603-4

y Jane Plowman, Leighton Buzzard
Great Britain by Bell and Bain Ltd, Glasgow

Contents

Acknowledgements iv

Introduction v

1 Language as Communication 1

2 The Developing Speaker and Listener 5

3 Addressing Communication Difficulties 14

4 A Policy for Language and Communication 23

5 Talk in the Literacy Hour 27

6 Communication Across the Curriculum 35

7 Talk in the Numeracy Hour 50

8 Organising Focused Language Activities 55

9 Using Resources Effectively 68

10 Assessing and Recording Speaking and Listening 82

Conclusion 95

Bibliography 97

Useful Addresses 99

Index 101

Acknowledgements

The author wishes to thank colleagues in Oldham, Lancashire, Hull and, in particular, those in the East Riding of Yorkshire, from whom information and many examples of good practice in developing speaking and listening have originated, and made this book possible.

Introduction

Speaking and listening are about language and communication. The correlation between children with under-developed language and poor achievement is widely accepted. Raised standards in literacy, numeracy and all areas of learning depend upon the attention also given to oracy in schools.

Speaking and Listening for All explores language as communication. It:

- places language in the context of the National Literacy Strategy and the National Numeracy Strategy;
- explores the development of speaking and listening skills;
- considers a school policy for speaking and listening;
- addresses language and communication difficulties;
- offers a range of practical classroom activities for developing speaking and listening across the curriculum; and
- explores the assessment and recording of pupils' language and communication.

Speaking and Listening for All will be welcomed by teachers at every key stage, in mainstream and special schools, as well as by students and other professionals in education. This book offers suggestions for developing language and communication to enhance learning and helps to promote raised standards across the curriculum.

Chapter 1

Language as Communication

Why do we speak and listen if the purpose is not to communicate? Can we even think without using language? The answer is far from simple. Consider the diagrams shown in Figure 1.1, and try to solve the two puzzles. Think about what is going through your mind as you do so. Are you thinking in images or words?

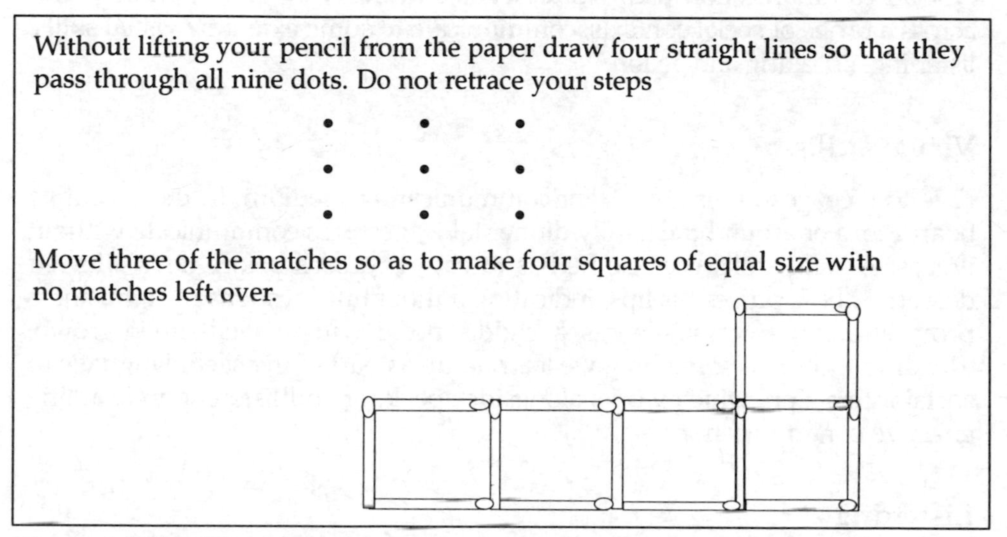

Figure 1.1 Thinking about language

Solving the problem is not important. What matters is the kind of thinking involved and the visual imagination and/or words which may have accompanied your thoughts. Clearly, we can solve some problems without using language. But can we communicate effectively without words? Can we reflect on the past, or consider the future? Can we develop ideas and plan projects? Bearing the above questions in mind may be helpful as the function of listening and speaking, in relation to learning, is explored. This book aims to show that words, and how to use them, are among the richest of gifts to children.

With whom do we communicate?

During the past week your communication may have included: members of the family; colleagues at work; parents or relatives of children taught; members of a club or focus of interest or people in the community, e.g. at the bank or the shops.

All communication has an audience which influences the words we use and how we deliver them as language. I speak to my husband each morning and evening, often about domestic issues. I attempt to converse with my three year old grand-daughter over the telephone, deliberately using language at her level of understanding. At weekends, I may talk with members of our local bowling club.

During the working day, teachers communicate with colleagues, pupils, and parents on teaching and learning issues as they arise. Staffrooms also act as social contexts for communication. The point of this reflection is the way in which effective language users adapt their content, tone and speed of language in order to reach a specific audience.

Why do we communicate?

Language has a purpose and a function. Browne (1996) lists many reasons for listening and speaking, in and out of school. These include the need to instruct, suggest, question, challenge, clarify, describe, discuss, explore understanding, initiate action or change, investigate, reflect, reshape thinking, rehearse experiences, speculate, state opinions, summarise, report and explain.

Readers may well amend or add to this list. The tone and delivery of speaking and listening also varies according to the audience. Instructions for a child to sit down and stop wandering around the classroom are likely to vary from a reminder to a colleague concerning an overdue report.

Some contexts for communication require more measured choices of vocabulary than others, e.g. a description to the police of items missing following a burglary.

How do we communicate?

Not all communication uses words. People at every stage of maturity, and across a range of social contexts, communicate to some extent by visual skills, listening, speaking and action.

Visual skills

Face to face, gesture is a constant communicating medium. In the executive boardroom or around the family dinner table, gestures communicate without words. A child sulks because he has to eat his greens before he is allowed dessert. A boss purses his lips, indicating a thoughtful response to a business proposition. A teacher silences a child's noise with a well-aimed frown. 'Reading' people is something we learn to do as part of the silent language of social interaction, which works alongside speaking and listening in enabling effective communication.

Listening

How often do teachers complain that children fail to listen? Listening is an integral part of communication. Consider the following contexts for listening:

- distinguishing between sounds, such as the doorbell, bird-song, aeroplanes overhead, running water, dogs barking; and
- discriminating between human interaction, such as shouting, crying or whispering.

The school day contains many different listening contexts. For example, pupils are required to:

- distinguish between letter sounds and clusters as part of their developing phonological awareness;
- listen to stories read to them;
- listen to instructions and respond appropriately;
- listen and respond to peers during group work;
- listen carefully during shared reading and writing, and word work during the literacy hour;
- listen to and respond in whole-class interaction;
- infer different shades of meaning from the tone and pitch of what is said;
- answer questions from teacher or peers; and
- judge the validity of what is heard.

There is more to listening than meets the eyes, or the ears.

Speaking

Talking with others is something most people do without thinking; but speaking has many dimensions. The range of functions for school talk are diverse; through the course of a single day, children may:

- answer the register at the appropriate time, and in the correct manner;
- talk about what they have done at home;
- explain to the teacher why a playtime argument occurred;
- request the use of a crayon, rubber or ruler from peers;
- discuss a piece of writing with an adult;
- analyse the results of a science experiment to demonstrate understanding;
- take part in a play for the whole school during assembly;
- speak in turn during a group game;
- indicate lunch time preferences to the dinner lady;
- ask for a paper towel to mop up a spill; or
- deliver a message to a teacher in another classroom.

Action

Actions communicate alone, or may accompany words. Consider the following:

- using body language or facial expression to convey a mood;
- a pupil ignoring the teacher's stern frown and continuing to exhibit inappropriate behaviour;
- using mime and dance effectively;
- thrusting a completed report angrily at the person who has requested it; and
- making models, and producing diagrammatic information.

The integration of visual skills, listening, speaking and actions illustrates communication as multi-sensory, with implications for the classroom. The effective communicator uses all four channels to achieve the required outcome from a social situation: a course tutor watches his audience as he speaks to judge their reactions, listens carefully and responds to questions, and uses gestures and expressions to accompany his words.

Language skills and strategies

The efficient language user needs both skills and strategies if language is to work effectively as a communicative tool. Consider the following as language skills:

- adequate knowledge of vocabulary;
- knowledge of grammar;
- knowledge of different language registers, e.g. the difference between classroom talk and playground chatter;
- knowledge of standard English.

Without the skills and knowledge of how words and sentences work together, neither speaking nor listening can communicate effectively. But language alone is not enough. The same words become an order, a request, or a statement depending on how they are delivered, e.g. with cutting sarcasm or a patient smile. 'Come here' may mean something different depending on whether we are speaking to a lover or a naughty child.

The language user relies also on a range of strategies to achieve his or her required outcome. Consider the following as strategies for using language skills:

- knowing when to listen and when to speak;
- balancing own communicating needs with those of others;
- judging the social context, i.e. the degree of formality;
- adapting language to suit the skills or status of the audience (younger children or the boss); and
- judging the tone of delivery – sarcastic, softly pleading.

Whatever the situation, effective communicators achieve their required outcome by judging their audience and coordinating both their choice of words and their delivery.

Goals and opportunities for language learners

Reflecting on the use of language and the attributes of effective speakers and listeners emphasises the fundamental importance of language as a learning tool. If children are to develop as language users, they must have opportunities to develop their speaking and listening skills; communicate with a range of audiences; and use language for different purposes and functions.

The general requirements of *English in the National Curriculum* (DfE 1995a) for children at Key Stages 1–4 state that, 'To develop effective speaking and listening skills, pupils should be taught to:

- use the vocabulary and grammar of standard English;
- formulate, clarify and express their ideas;
- adapt their speech to a widening range of circumstances and demands; and
- listen, understand and respond appropriately to others.'

The role of language as a means of understanding ourselves and others is also important. Effective speaking and listening skills enable learners, as they mature, to:

- connect with and extend their world;
- feel good about themselves and build up self-esteem;
- feel secure and confident in a range of social contexts;
- develop the confidence to extend learning beyond school; and
- develop attitudes and skills for independent learning.

The Plowden Report (DfE 1967) stressed the importance of the child at the centre of learning:

> Children have to be themselves, to learn from their environment, to enjoy the present, to get ready for the future, to create and to love, to learn, to face adversity, to behave responsibly, to be human beings.

Many of the suggestions from this report are echoed in current educational philosophy: for example, the central role of children in their own learning and the involvement of pupils with SEN in their Individual Education Plans (IEPs) and reviews.

Language and literacy

As communication tools, language and literacy are interdependent: as the channels for listening and reading are receptive, those for speaking and writing are productive. All areas of communication relate to thinking and understanding.

The inter-relationship of language skills and their joint development poses challenges for educators. All four strands of English need to develop together, if they are to enrich each other. As the National Curriculum (NC) for English further states, 'English should develop pupils' abilities to communicate effectively in speech and writing, and to listen with understanding. It should also enable them to be enthusiastic and knowledgeable readers.'

The role of English in the National Curriculum as schools continue to grapple with the National Literacy Strategy (DfEE 1998b) needs to be questioned. The NLS cannot deliver all of the experiences and opportunities necessary for children to become effective communicators. What happens in English lessons, the literacy hour and across different subject areas must be coordinated if communication for all children is the ultimate aim.

Chapter 2

The Developing Speaker and Listener

There is a marked difference in the development of language *per se* and the development of competency in speaking and listening. Children can develop their language without developing the strategies which enable them to use it. At its simplest, language involves the gradual acquisition of words and sentence structures. Learning to receive language through listening and to produce language through speech is a long way from being an effective speaker and listener in context.

How often have you listened with rapt attention to a captivating speaker on a course, and marvelled at how well that speaker held the audience's attention? Most of us have experienced meetings which have been cleverly manipulated by individuals who presented the most persuasive arguments. Consider also the persuasive speaking, if not listening, accomplishments of most politicians. Becoming a language user relies on learning how and when to speak and listen in a range of social situations. The first sections of this chapter explore communicative behaviour, and are followed by a brief look at language elements.

Initial communication

Communication begins at birth. Babies respond to a range of sounds and gradually develop concepts of the world around them. Touch, smell and taste, as well as hearing and sight, contribute to concept development. At its earliest stages, concept formation could be described as an inner awareness of an idea or an object which is continued when the object is not there. It starts with the awareness of permanence; the realisation that an object is the same and continues to exist when it is out of sight.

An understanding of familiar and recurring situations follows. A child responds to, 'Shall we sit you in the high chair?' with a beaming smile, realising a meal is imminent, though the words themselves have no meaning to the child. The language is meaningful only as a sequence of familiar events. Symbolic understanding accompanies play which represents familiar situations, e.g. dolls are given lunch, or got ready for bed. Once symbols are understood, verbalising can begin.

Receptive language

Comprehension of language precedes its production and has many implications for the classroom. Children who arrive in school without adequate conceptual knowledge must understand what is presented before they can assimilate it and use it as language. Children understand more than they can express; therefore it is always difficult to assess how much language children have actually acquired.

How does understanding grow?

Put simply, receptive understanding of language progresses through the following sequence:

1. Vocabulary – children learn to name objects and actions, and develop a receptive understanding of nouns and verbs – ball, teddy, pudding, spoon, eat, bath, play, raining. Adjectives and prepositions – words of colour, shape and feel, and words of position – are acquired.

2. Grammatical understanding – children begin to respond to sentences of increasing length and complexity.
3. Different grammatical forms – understanding of more precise grammatical forms develops, e.g. word endings, verb tenses and pronouns.

As their language is developing, children are also starting to appreciate its effect upon their lives, i.e. its varying functions:

- instruction – put your toys away;
- information – Grandma's coming to tea;
- question – do you want some milk?

Expressive language

For the majority of children expressive language follows from receptive understanding. Expressive language means the ability to combine words into different phrases and sentences and to convey meaning through them. Children must understand words and phrases before they can be expected to use them.

The functions of language already explored illustrate how we learn language in many different ways.

How does expressive language develop?

For the majority of children there is a sequence of progression. The first words often appear between nine and 18 months. Children learn to express themselves through:

1. Single words – this may signify a need, e.g. a favourite toy to go to sleep with.
2. Two words – the child may represent Mother coming through the door with 'Mummy home'. By about the second year, most children are starting to string words together. Brown (1973) analysed the grammatical elements of language which may appear at about the age of two. These are listed in Figure 2.1.
3. Longer phrases – Mother arriving through the door may be expressed as 'Mummy come home'.
4. Simple structures – these usually contain meaning carrying words (bath, television, orange juice) and omit function words (in, the, and).
5. Sentences – these gradually increase in complexity. Children learn to connect simple sentences, often by the over use of 'and'. How familiar is, 'we went to see Grandad and we had some fish and chips and we went to the zoo and . . . '? The use of tenses allows an emerging language user to relate past and present events. The use of the future tense allows the child to predict his thoughts forwards, e.g. by saying what he wants for Christmas, or where he is going on holiday.

The difference between 'I know Dad got a letter and now we're going to Glasgow', and 'It was only when I heard what had happened that I realised they had sent the letter,' illustrates the complexities of grammar and the inherent difficulties for children and teachers. Utterances at the level of complexity illustrated by the second sentence are not achieved at all by many children.

Children can only develop language if a competent language user is there to interpret their world, and to put regular routines and happenings into words for them to understand and learn to express with ever-increasing complexity.

. . . went home. Train coming. In fridge. On table. Dogs run away. That Daddy's. Are they boys? I got a book. I saw the policeman. Dolly jumped. He runs fast. Does it hurt? Are you coming? Is Daddy waiting? That's a giraffe. They're going away.

Figure 2.1 Grammatical features from about two years of age, from *A First Language: The Early Stages* (Brown 1973)

Implications for the classroom

Research suggests that the majority of children acquire an impressive amount of language before they arrive at school. By the age of five, most have mastered the basic meanings and grammar of their community and are ready to develop their language in the school context, and to learn to read and write.

The barriers for those children who have not acquired language are overwhelming, with massive implications in the classroom context. Such children cannot follow instructions, ask questions, say they want to go to the toilet, and so on. A language programme must be initiated to enable the child to function effectively and to learn. The above description of early language development illustrates how the language disadvantaged child will flounder at every stage of learning without planned concept development and grammar teaching as a preparation for oral or literacy activities.

Working towards the National Curriculum

A document from the Qualifications and Curriculum Authority (QCA) and the DfEE (DfEE/QCA 1998) provides a useful analysis of the stages of communication leading up to the early years curriculum. The small steps of progression support the target-setting process in special and mainstream schools, but are relevant here to illustrate levels of communicative behaviour for what is commonly referred to as 'working towards' the National Curriculum attainment levels.

Figure 2.2 plots small steps of communicative behaviour from the earliest level of P1, beyond which some pupils with profound or very severe learning difficulties may not progress.

P1. Shows sensory awareness related to people or objects; shows reflex responses to sensory stimuli.

P2. Performs some actions and reactive responses – smiling, turning or holding.

P3. Shows anticipation in response to familiar people or routines and responds appropriately; explores and manipulates objects or toys; communicates simple choices, likes or dislikes, e.g. by pointing or gestures; babble, using different tones and sounds, with vocalised gestures to communicate.

Figure 2.2 Early communicative behaviour, adapted from *Supporting the Target Setting Process – Guidance for Effective Target Setting for Pupils with Special Educational Needs* (DfEE/QCA 1998)

Figure 2.3 combines speaking/expression with listening/comprehension to show the small steps of progression from P4 to P8 of the QCA/DfEE document, and provides us with attainment descriptions of communicative behaviour and first steps in language. The targets also represent the attainment of children with severe language retardation on arrival at nursery, and many children with severe language difficulties in special schools.

Early years

The early years child is identified in this context as one who attends an educational establishment leading up to Key Stage 1, i.e. nursery and reception level. During these foundation years, children are building on what they have already learned, through carefully planned and focused play activities. During the early years of education children are further developing:

- language concepts and grammar;
- a range of social skills;
- auditory discrimination; and
- visual discrimination.

P4. Makes representational sounds (brmm, brmm when playing with a toy car); uses a range of single words, gestures, signs or symbols; repeats, copies or imitates words or phrases; follows single-step instructions; shows understanding of names of familiar objects.

P5. Combines two or more ideas or concepts, e.g. more drink; combines two/three words, signs or symbols to communicate meaning to range of listeners; beginning to listen and respond . . . to simple questions about familiar events; follows range of one step messages or instructions.

P6. Uses clear words, gestures and signs to enhance or clarify communication; uses facial expression to enhance meanings; uses phrases to communicate simple ideas/events/stories; asks simple questions; responds to two-step messages or instructions; responds appropriately to others in small group.

P7. Uses phrases and statements to communicate ideas, recount events or experiences; sometimes adds new information beyond what is asked; contributes appropriately – in pairs, groups and role-play; follows stories, messages and instructions; responds in a pair or small group – minimum adult support.

P8. Communicates ideas and experiences in larger groups; uses growing vocabulary to convey meaning; makes up own stories; takes part in role-play with confidence; listens attentively in larger groups; listens and responds to stories, songs, nursery rhymes and poems.

Figure 2.3 First steps in language, adapted from *Supporting the Target Setting Process – Guidance for Effective Target Setting for Pupils with Special Educational Needs* (DfEE/QCA 1998)

The desirable outcomes

Looking at Children's Learning (SCAA 1997) specified 'desirable outcomes' as goals for learning on entering compulsory education. These provide a foundation for learning across the subjects of the National Curriculum, and are intended to be delivered through an integrated, exciting and multi-sensory range of learning experiences.

A Framework for the Primary Curriculum (NCC 1989a), also reflects the principles upon which an early years curriculum is founded:

- learning starts from children's current level of understanding and the experiences each child brings to the learning context;
- learning should be relevant to a child's environment and social context;
- children progress towards independence through age-appropriate choices and learning related responsibilities; and
- cross-curricular approaches enhance and develop children's perceptions of the environment.

Structured and language-based play provides the foundations for early learning. Figure 2.4 states the language section of the desirable outcomes for language and literacy which indicate what children should have achieved in language by the time they start compulsory education.

> *Language section*
> In small and large groups, children listen attentively and talk about their experiences. They use a growing vocabulary with increasing fluency to express thoughts and convey meaning to their listeners. They listen and respond to stories, songs, nursery rhymes and poems. They make up their own stories and take part in role-play with confidence.

Figure 2.4 'Desirable outcomes' for language and literacy, from *Looking at Children's Learning* (SCAA 1997)

Correlation between the later stages (P7 and P8) of the QCA/DfEE targets for 'working towards', and the desirable outcomes for language and literacy reflect the essential role of focused and planned talk at the starting point of education. Children need to see and hear positive models of language and communicative behaviour and be guided towards using their own communication skills for a range of functions and audiences.

Links with the NLS

Through their early years, children need to develop:
- auditory discrimination skills – variations in a range of sounds – objects, animals, humans – leading to differences in sounds of words and letters;
- visual discrimination skills – using pictures and shapes to find the odd one out, which are similar and different etc. – leading to seeing differences between words and letters;
- their abilities to work appropriately in different sizes of groups; and
- their skills in using language to convey meaning to different audiences for varying functions.

Samples from the *National Literacy Strategy (NLS): Framework for Teaching* (DfEE 1998b) objectives for reading and writing at reception level show how pupils should be progressing from the earlier 'working towards' stages of communicative behaviour and language use. Pupils should be taught:

1. *Vocabulary extension*
   - new words from their reading and shared experiences; and
   - to make collections of . . . personal interest and significant words.
2. *Phonological awareness*
   - to understand and be able to rhyme . . . ; and
   - hearing and identifying initial sounds in words and dominant phonemes.
3. *Grammatical awareness*
   - to expect written text to make sense and to check for sense if it does not; and
   - to use awareness of the grammar of a sentence to predict words during shared reading.
4. *Understanding of print and reading comprehension*
   - understand and use correctly terms about books and print – book, cover, word, letter etc.; and
   - understand how story book language works.
5. *Understanding of print and writing composition*
   - understand that writing can be used a range of purposes i.e. to send messages, record, inform . . . ; and
   - to think about and discuss what they intend to write ahead of writing it.

The objectives listed illustrate how the foundations of language and communicative behaviour described, facilitate achievement of the NLS objectives for reading and writing, and other learning. Without auditory discrimination children cannot identify rhyme and alliteration. Without spoken language children cannot develop grammatical awareness. Without having played and talked as members of different groups, children are less likely to produce the communicative behaviour necessary for achievement in reading comprehension and writing composition.

Speaking and listening at Key Stage 1

The language and communicative behaviour already described enable children to step onto the National Curriculum attainment ladder for listening and speaking, the majority of children being expected to reach Level 2 by the time they leave Key Stage 1.

Following on from the 'working towards' breakdown of early years speaking and listening, the QCA/DfEE document also includes a breakdown of National Curriculum Levels 1 and 2 which may help schools to plan and implement small step programmes of oral work for children whose progress in speaking and listening will need to be carefully charted.

Figure 2.5 shows the three-step breakdown, and progression, for National Curriculum Level 1 starting from the simplest step, 1C, and followed by the National Curriculum attainment description for Level 1 (DfE 1995a). The targets reflect the DfEE/QCA (1998) document.

Pupils:

1C communicate . . . matters of interest in familiar settings;
understand and respond appropriately to simple comments or instructions directed at them; and
convey meanings, with some relevant details, to range of others.

1B communicate clearly about matters of interest to individuals and groups;
follow what others say and respond appropriately to simple instructions directed at them; and
convey meaning, making what they communicate relevant and interesting to the listener.

1A communicate clearly about matters of interest, taking turns in a range of situations and groups;
follow what others say and usually respond appropriately; and
convey meaning, sustaining their contribution and the listener's interest.

National Curriculum Level 1 attainment description – Pupils talk about matters of immediate interest. They listen to others and usually respond appropriately. They convey simple meanings to a range of listeners, speaking audibly, and begin to extend their ideas or accounts by providing some detail.

Figure 2.5 National Curriculum Level 1 – three-step breakdown, from *English in the National Curriculum* (DfE 1995a)

For children with language and communication difficulties, the key differences between each step may need to be specifically developed. For example, simply 'understanding and responding' (1C) is a step behind the need to 'follow what others say' (1B). Similarly, 'sustaining their contribution' and 'taking turns in a range of situations and groups' (1A) represents a significant leap forward in communicative behaviour for many children.

Figure 2.6 represents a similar three-step breakdown for National Curriculum Level 2. Analysis of the three steps is significant. For example, 'different responses' (2C) represents a growing awareness of audience. At step 2B, this has become 'adaptation . . . to suit the needs of the person', demonstrating a growing move away from the self. By 2A there is a recognition of formal and informal situations, illustrating the need for children to further differentiate their role according to the formality of the situation. This is a big step for many children. As well as facilitating schools' recognition of smaller steps of achievement for children whose language progression needs to be carefully monitored, these breakdowns also identify the minute differences which make communication appear effective or ineffective, and behaviour appropriate or inappropriate.

Links with the NLS – Years 1 and 2

The requirements of the NLS Framework objectives for Years 1 and 2 rest firmly on the communication elements explored so far. It is through focused and planned talk that children are able to develop their phonological awareness and phonic knowledge, their grammatical awareness and their comprehension and skills in writing composition.

Pupils:

2C communicate with peers and adults in a range of situations about topics of interest to them;
are aware of need for different responses depending on people or situation; and
explain their ideas and respond directly to what others have said.

2B communicate ideas or experiences with increasing detail in a range of situations;
show some adaptation of their responses to suit the needs of the person they are communicating with, choosing appropriate vocabulary; and
make a range of contributions in groups.

2A show confidence in communicating ideas, using a growing vocabulary, and responding appropriately to others in a range of situations, particularly where the topics interest them; and
show awareness of needs of listener and adapt communication accordingly, e.g. in formal and informal situations.

National Curriculum Level 2 attainment target – Pupils begin to show confidence in talking and listening, particularly where the topics interest them. On occasions they show awareness of the needs of the listener by including relevant detail. In develop ing and explaining their ideas, they speak clearly and use a growing vocabulary. They usually listen carefully, and respond with increasing appropriate- ness to what others say. They are beginning to be aware that in some situations a more formal vocabulary and tone of voice are used.

Figure 2.6 National Curriculum Level 2 – three-step breakdown, from *English in the National Curriculum* (DfE 1995a)

If children are to be taught 'new words from reading and shared experiences, and to make collections of . . . words' (NLS Year 1), and to 'build individual collections' (NLS Year 2), then speaking and listening become the media through which this growing vocabulary emerges as language. New words become usable only when they are secured as concepts, added to pupils' increasing repertoire and manipulated as language, for the benefit of the speaker and the listener, in the range of social contexts already explored.

Speaking and listening at Key Stage 2

The competent listener and speaker has progressed a long way from the early beginnings explored in this chapter. Children who have not acquired the foundations of language and communicative behaviour so far described will struggle to keep up with the Key Stage 2 curriculum, and the in-depth requirements of the NLS Framework for Years 3 to 6, which build onto those of Key Stage 1. Figure 2.7 lists the key phrases of speaking and listening from National Curriculum Levels 3 and 4 which illustrate progression through Key Stage 2.

The Level 4 speaker and listener coordinates speaking and listening in order to be 'responsive to other's ideas and views,' and has moved a long way from using language simply to respond to personal needs.

Speaking and listening at secondary school and beyond

By Key Stages 3 and 4, the combined use of language with the kind of communicative behaviour which enables cross-curricular learning is of paramount importance. Pupils have to cope with many different teachers and styles of teaching and learning, and the role of talk may change from lesson to lesson. Pupils are presented with a range of new vocabulary. Even friendships may suddenly cease and new ones start. Such immense changes require confidence and some degree of independence in the Year 7 pupil having to find his way in what may appear to be a strange new world.

Pupils at NC Level 3:
- talk, listen confidently . . . explore, communicate ideas;
- adapt . . . to needs of listener . . . vary use of vocabulary . . . level of detail;
- begin to be aware of standard English . . . when it is used.

Pupils at NC Level 4:
- talk and listen . . . increasing range of contexts;
- talk is adapted to the purpose;
- listen carefully . . . responsive to others' ideas/views; and
- use appropriately some of the features . . . of standard English vocabulary and grammar.

Figure 2.7 Speaking and listening at National Curriculum Levels 3 and 4

Imagine the problem for children whose language and communication are underdeveloped. They may be too shy to ask questions in class and leave lessons unable to understand the vocabulary, which often means they cannot do their homework. Alternatively, a child with a stammer may be unable to ask the way to a new classroom for fear of being laughed at by other pupils. For many children with poor communication skills, the secondary school may appear a frightening place.

Beyond Level 4 of the NC, speaking and listening develop in the following ways. A child should:
- be confident in a wide range of contexts . . . some of a formal nature;
- engage interest of listener;
- take account of other's views;
- use standard English in formal situations;
- adapt talk to the demands of different contexts;
- take active part in discussion . . . [and show] sensitivity to others; and
- have fluent use of standard English in formal situations.

The mature speaker and listener has the tools for taking part in a wide range of social situations beyond school. For example, having joined our local art society knowing very little about art I had to acquire the terminology used by long-standing members before I could join in any talk about the techniques.

Language is far more than words and sentences: without language, speaking and listening cannot happen. Progression through the stages of communicative behaviour depends on language as the medium through which effective communication is achieved.

What language do learners need?

In order to function as a social being, i.e. to communicate, and to progress as learners, children need:
- knowledge of language used around school;
- knowledge of language in the home and the environment;
- the language of books and reading – page, word, cover, pictures, beginning, end, top, bottom, story etc.;
- the meaning-carrying vocabulary of reading schemes;
- the language of writing – pencil, crayon, paper etc.;
- the language of maths - more than, difference, number;

- the vocabulary and concepts presented through shared texts used in the literacy hour;
- concepts necessary for independence in the literacy hour;
- cross-curricular vocabulary required for each topic;
- understanding of the vocabulary in stories read to them; and
- the language of games – taking turns, first, second, share out, pairs, turn over, face down, match etc.

Strategies for developing the above, and suggestions for addressing language difficulties, feature in further chapters.

Language elements

Finally, this chapter will consider the elements of language which enable communication. Figure 2.8 lists elements of language which, for some children, could represent their learning targets. The list may suggest an approximate progression, but is not intended as a rigid sequence.

1. Names self, familiar objects and happenings – own names, parts of body, family, toys, school objects, routines;
2. Uses simple prepositions;
3. Uses identifying statements e.g. It's a table;
4. Describes items, e.g. using colour, size, shape;
5. Follows one-step instructions, e.g. Put your pencils down;
6. Describes actions of self and others at phrase level and simple sentence level.
7. Includes negative forms;
8. Uses simple question forms;
9. Uses regular plural forms;
10. Uses irregular plural forms;
11. Follows two-step instructions;
12. Uses pronouns correctly;
13. Uses simple sentences to: describe components of familiar objects, e.g. a toy car; state activity sequences, e.g. the order of the school day, the sequence of the PE lesson; explain the function of an object, activity or event, e.g. what a computer is used for; state materials needed for an activity; and make comparisons.
14. Uses basic verb tenses – present, past and future;
15. Categorises objects, events and people, as basic sets, e.g. animals, fruits, flowers, shapes; and as sub-sets, e.g. wild or domestic animals.
16. Uses more complex structures, possibly containing: a wider range of connectives, e.g. while, although; negatives other than 'not'; more complex question words and forms, e.g. whose; extensive use of pronouns; refined use of verb structures, e.g. conditional tenses; consequential thinking –what if . . . ?; and backward-references, e.g. The train screeched to a halt. At that point . . .
17. Includes a range of abstract, usually multi-syllabic, vocabulary, e.g. words which have only textual meaning, e.g. available, indication, specific, enclosed, minor etc.

Figure 2.8 Elements of language

Many of the elements of language listed in Figure 2.8 could apply at any stage of learning. Pupils developing subject vocabulary at secondary level will need to name tools and objects before they can describe them or state their function. The list is intended to support schools in identifying targets for focused language work.

This chapter has explored two related strands of growth – language skills, and the communicative behaviour which accompanies them. Competency in speaking and listening requires the coordination of both.

Chapter 3

Addressing Communication Difficulties

Dealing with communication difficulties implies that the source of difficulty must be understood and teased out by teachers in order to address the problems through the right strategies and resources. The majority of speaking and listening problems are dealt with in the mainstream classroom, through a rich learning environment, possibly supplemented with sensitive and well-focused intervention where appropriate. Many initial language difficulties are outgrown as children mature.

Browne (1996) comments that teachers' references to 'poor language' are often used in a general sense to describe children who have difficulty with listening attentively; following instructions; responding to questions; speaking clearly; or using standard English.

Children with the type of classroom-based problems identified above may progress with little more than differentiated strategies and resources which allow them to use learning opportunities to the full. These communication difficulties may stem from underdeveloped language skills, a lack of required communicative behaviour, or both.

A further group of children may exhibit 'poor language' which stems from a sensory impairment, or from one of a variable range of severe language disorders. Where the difficulties are severe, intervention may mean plotting the language and the communicative behaviour of individual children, or groups, against a developmental scale in order to implement a language programme, i.e. as part of an Individual Educational Plan (IEP). This chapter explores communication difficulties from both perspectives.

Communication problems in the classroom

Observation over time may identify many of the behaviours outlined in the following sections.

Problems in understanding language

Children may not do as they are told; lose concentration; fail to follow instructions; wander around the room; seek reassurance from adults; respond inappropriately or need frequent clarification of what to do.

What can teachers do?

Children who do not understand what is being said will often appear lost and unable to 'place themselves' within the social interaction of the nursery or Key Stage 1 environment. The following strategies may help:

- use clear and simple structures, without sounding unnatural;
- be consistent with regular verbal routines, e.g. taking the register, or giving instructions;
- talk about what is relevant, giving language both context and immediacy, and extend the range of contexts in a meaningful way;
- repeat and rephrase if necessary, e.g. in allocating tasks;
- use gesture with the words to aid understanding;
- engage the pupil's attention before speaking – to look and listen; and
- focus on the delivery, using the required intonation – e.g. instruction, question, statement.

Children with very limited understanding of language may also require a programme of intervention, incorporating a precise sequence of skill areas, delivered in context as far as possible: for example, the language of shopping may require a trip into a shop, with focused use of stated nouns and verbs as part of the language extension programme.

Expressive language difficulties

Children may demonstrate their understanding of language but fail to produce it. Their difficulties could be manifested in any number of ways. Pupils may:

- possess the vocabulary and structures but not use them;
- talk about unrelated topics, e.g. in a history lesson the child suddenly tells you what he did the night before;
- repeat what has been said instead of responding to it;
- struggle to find the right word to respond with;
- be reluctant to answer a question; or
- only use phrases, or use sentences with incorrect grammar.

What can be done?

Firstly, tease out the source of the problem. If lack of language is evident, a specific programme to identify language elements is necessary. If a lack of communicative behaviour is the likely cause, then focused opportunities to engage in speaking and listening with different sizes and combinations of groups may be what children need.

Praise for even one word will also encourage the reluctant speaker to respond and express himself through speech. Poor self-esteem and confidence in social situations may be the problem.

The poor listener

Assuming that children have the required levels of language, listening may simply need to be trained. Poor listeners may exhibit tendencies such as:

- indicating that what is said is 'rubbish' (especially older less able pupils);
- switching off from listening and speaking activities;
- not following stories;
- not doing as instructed; or
- hearing, but not responding to what is heard.

Strategies to address poor listening

These could include:

- ensuring that listening has a purpose and requires a response from the listener;
- engaging children's attention before speaking;
- delivering speech clearly and with good eye contact;
- informing children in advance what they are to listen to or for, e.g. the task to follow, or questions about a story;
- reducing distractions where possible, e.g. computer noise;
- drawing activities from listening which focus on detail (Draw a square. Put three circles inside. Colour one circle green and two red);
- taped activities of all kinds, e.g. taped stories, taped instructions, simulated telephone conversations — to enhance use of the ears and minimise use of the eyes; and
- checking out individual attention now and again, e.g. by asking questions in between oral interaction, and telling children at the start that you are going to do so.

Giving listening a clear, communicated purpose and a focus can often address the problem.

The child who rarely speaks

Many children rarely take part in oral work. They have the necessary language but do not use it for varied reasons. They do not volunteer any news, and show reluctance to talk about personal experiences in general. Such children may lack confidence in class discussion, feeling that their contribution is not good enough; feel ashamed of their home and therefore refuse to bring 'home issues' into school; or simply lack experience in social situations.

Ideas to try out:

Such children need encouragement to speak in no-fail situations, e.g. to respond to questions where the answer will not be wrong. If incorrect, it is important that their responses are not instantly dismissed, but clearly shown as partly right, and a good try. Many less able children become wary of putting their hand up to answer if their response receives a simple 'No'.

Role-play may encourage reluctant speakers to talk 'in character' and gradually enable them to talk as themselves. Hand puppets and masks, or dressing up, may make children less self-conscious. Acting out common problems or social issues may elicit communication from children whose troubles often prevent them from speaking.

The over-dominant speaker

Some children talk too much, preventing others from joining in the conversation. Dominant speakers have not learned when to speak and when to listen, and may not have acquired turn-taking skills. They can ruin the interactive nature of group work, and force reluctant speakers into a passive role. Strategies to address the problem include:

- playing games where turn-taking is a feature;
- the speaker holding a small, soft ball, which focuses group attention on who is speaking and who is listening;
- building up a group story or piece of writing, with contributions in turn;
- expressing the need to talk by putting a hand up, discouraging interruptions; and
- giving a dominant talker a different role in group work, e.g. as a scribe.

The shy child

Shy pupils can only overcome their shyness by taking part in a range of talking activities, with different peers. If a shy child works only with a 'best friend' the shyness is unlikely to be conquered. Such children need sensitive encouragement to work in different ways, for different purposes.

The shy child may be easily 'squashed' in a group, especially if another child is dominating the talk. Group activities which encourage children to be assertive without being aggressive help all children to develop communication skills. Assertiveness training could include:

- discussions of polite and impolite behaviour;
- simulations of good models of turn-taking;
- showing children ways of interjecting into a group without interrupting others in mid-flow;
- showing children how to assert themselves politely, using the right words and gestures; and
- making self-confidence a priority.

The incoherent speaker

How often have you told a child to slow down and think because his speech is fragmented and disordered, making it difficult for the listener to grasp his meaning? Encourage more thoughtful speech by:

- asking the child to recount the day's events;
- drawing attention to sequence, e.g. beginnings and ends of stories;
- asking children to describe a picture, focusing on one part at a time;
- working with simple recipes, using sequenced activities; and
- remodelling incoherent speech by repeating it in a more appropriate way.

The child who rarely questions

Children who always accept what is said and rarely question, or seek to clarify information, will not develop the interrogation skills needed as they get older. Some may understand what they hear, but do not evaluate it. All children need to develop questioning skills and strategies as part of their communication, and to develop assertiveness in large group situations. Encourage positive questioning by:

- offering praise for thoughtful questioning;
- pair work – children asking each other questions;
- debating on current issues which encourages children to question each other's points of view;
- surveying and interview tasks;
- group or class riddles – to be solved only by questions;
- drawing attention to questions in text work, and ensure children know what questions are for; and
- using odd moments to present a question word starter – what, where, when, who or why – for one child to turn into a question, and another child to answer it.

Alternative dialects and accents

Standard English forms part of the Key Skills of *English in the National Curriculum* (DfE 1995a) and appears in the NLS Framework for Teaching as 'grammatical awareness'. The general requirements for English at Key Stages 1–4 state that:

> In order to speak confidently in public, cultural and working life, pupils need to be able to speak, write and read standard English fluently and accurately . . . The richness of dialects . . . can make an important contribution to pupils' knowledge and understanding of standard English.

The Key Skills for Key Stage 1 speaking and listening further comment that:

> Pupils should be introduced with appropriate sensitivity to . . . standard English . . . and given opportunities to consider their own speech and how they communicate with others. Pupils should . . . recognise how language differs.

Dialect differs from accent. Dialect represents regional variations, mainly of verb agreements, in particular the verb 'to be'. Accent reflects pronunciation differences, e.g. Scottish, Welsh, Irish or English and, within those, Lancashire, Yorkshire and so on. Attitudes to alternative dialects and accents affect the way in which individuals are perceived and, in certain social circles, may influence how far persons without standard English speech are 'accepted'.

The Cornish child arriving at a Yorkshire school may bring with him a delightfully alternative way of speaking. The Lancashire or Yorkshire child arriving at a London school may well take with him many dialectical and accent variations. The extract in Figure 3.1 shows a pupil's awareness of dialect and accent. All pupils need to feel comfortable about their own speech and recognise it as different but not inferior. At the same time, they need to recognise the need for standard English in formal situations.

'When I'm in company and relations come, or mostly at home, I pronounce my words properly. Like – "watter" – instead of saying that like I sometimes do at school, I say "water" and "I'm gooin," I say "I'm going".'
'What would happen if you were talking to your mates and you said "water" instead of "watter"?'
'They'd think, er, "Ay up . . . funny feller".'
'Why?'
'Cause it's community – the Grimethorpe community.'
'What do you mean?'
'Well, we all talk with one general accent and we expect everybody else to talk like it, and if they don't talk – you know, like posh n'all – we all think er . . .'
'– e's a ponce!'
'Yeh!'

Figure 3.1 Pupil's awareness of speech difference (Extract from a discussion at Mile End House School, Grimethorpe, Yorkshire, broadcast by the BBC as part of *2nd House*, 2nd January 1975)

This section has focused on communication issues which do not necessarily have a special educational need (SEN) source, and for which the desired standard of speaking and listening can be encouraged or trained within, and as a part of, the mainstream curriculum. The following section focuses attention on more specific language and communication difficulties, many of which require specialist intervention.

Specialised language and communication difficulties

The focus on desirable outcomes in the early years, combined with baseline assessment as children enter compulsory education, provides initial indicators of children whose language and communication difficulties require specialised intervention. The following sections aim to clarify some of the main specialised areas of communication difficulty.

Verbal dyspraxia

Connery (1987) describes dyspraxia as a 'difficulty with learned patterns of movement'. The child with verbal/articulatory dyspraxia has problems with coordinating the precise movements necessary for clear speech, e.g. of the lips, tongue, soft palate, hard palate, larynx (voice box) and the muscles which control breathing for speech. Verbal dyspraxia may be the only dyspraxic problem for the child, or there could be other dyspraxias, causing other problems, e.g. handwriting.

Connery further stresses that the child with verbal dyspraxia will need specialised speech therapy and daily practice of speech exercises. The verbally dyspraxic child is likely to meet the criteria for placement in a language unit. The learning support assistant (LSA) who supports the child with speech exercises needs to be trained by a speech therapist.

The dyspraxic child may experience constant failure because of the unintelligible nature of his speech, and he needs to know that adults and peers understand his problems and are there to support him with time, patience and encouragement.

Dyslexia

Dyslexia is often portrayed as a disability, but may in fact represent a unique learning style. While all dyslexics have spelling, and to a large extent, reading and/or mathematical difficulties, many excel in speaking, listening, and particularly thinking skills. Children with dyslexia are likely to experience failure in literacy as they grapple with their problems, but can be encouraged to use their oral communication and creative talents to the full. Many dyslexics are holistic and visual thinkers and need to build on those skills to compensate for their literacy difficulties.

The hearing impaired (HI) child

Discussion with specialist colleagues in hearing impaired services has contributed to the following advice for addressing hearing impairment in mainstream classrooms. Hearing impairment may be in many forms: hearing loss may be anywhere between mild and profound; loss could be in the middle or the inner ear, and affects the sound of a word; children can be born deaf, or become deaf after acquiring language.

How we talk to children (and adults) with hearing impairment is important. One should:

- talk in a normal voice, without exaggeration;
- be still as you speak, and allow the person to see face and lip movements;
- cue the child in before you start to speak; and
- use objects or pictures as contextual clues.

In the literacy hour, for example, it would be important to turn to face the class, with the HI child in a central position, before speaking about what has been written down.

Certain kinds of words are harder for the HI child to receive. Names of people, places and things are hard to lip-read, and need to be written down. This is partly because they are less easily cued from the sentence context. Vowels are louder than consonants, and consonants at the end of words are the hardest for the HI child to detect. Some early phonic work, such as consonant digraphs — sh, ch and th — are hard to hear. It helps if the sound is written down.

Hearing aids are helpful but pick up every sound in the classroom, including those from the computer or Language Master. Hearing aids work best at a distance of one metre which has implications for where the HI child is to be seated during the literacy hour and other activities.

Language disorders

A semantic–pragmatic language disorder is one which concerns the meaning and the use of language. A semantic disorder relates to word meaning, and may affect a child's ability to deal with new vocabulary, categorisation, and other word associations. A pragmatic disorder affects the use of language, both receptive and expressive.

What are the implications for teachers?

A semantic–pragmatic language disorder may affect children in the following ways:

- inability to extract and retain meaning, e.g. from instructions;
- difficulties with mathematical language;
- difficulties in reading, spelling and independent writing;
- problems with describing and recording;
- difficulties with analysis and reasoning, and the 'how' and 'what if' uses of language; and
- difficulty in interpreting gestures and other non-verbal communication.

The child with such a disorder may not understand a joke because he cannot grasp word relationships and subtle nuances of meaning. A further example may be the child who can understand and respond to language in a concrete situation with visual stimuli, but appears lost when events are discussed separately from their context (e.g. home news discussed in school).

Children with semantic–pragmatic language disorders need to work intensively on:

- language form – speech and grammatical skills;
- content – word meanings and relationships; and
- language use – context and situation.

Sensitively focused work on vocabulary and grammar in the literacy hour will help children whose language difficulties fit into the above descriptions, in addition to a specialised intervention programme.

The language unit

Attendance at a language unit may be part of the intervention for children with the above disorders. Once assessed as needing specialist intervention, a child will be further assessed by a multi-disciplinary team, in order for a specific programme to be implemented. This should include:

- speech and language therapist – to assess the nature and extent of the language and communication problem;
- educational psychologist – to assess learning skills in relation to overall development;
- medical officer – to perform a medical examination and monitor overall development; and
- audiologist – to assess hearing.

Careful observation in the nursery and school, with reference to the development of language skills and strategies as explored in Chapter 2, should identify children whose language and communication is a cause for concern and may require specialist assessment and intervention.

Autistic spectrum disorders

Jordan, speaking on autistic spectrum disorders, at a conference in 1998, described the learning difficulties that arise from autism as, 'qualitative differences in cognitive, perceptual and emotional processes such as would constitute an autistic style of thinking and learning'. Effective education depends on understanding how the 'autistic' person learns and understands his world.

'Autistic' children require a curriculum, either in mainstream or in specialist provision, that is pupil-centred; prioritises communication skills; teaches cultural norms/meanings; teaches life skills; and has access to imitation/observation of non-autistic peers.

For mainstream teachers coping with a child with these difficulties, detailed support should be available, either from local education authority (LEA) or SEN services, or staff from an autistic unit, who may operate an outreach service.

Severe learning difficulties (SLD)

To teach children with SLD to communicate, we need to be guided by the stages of language acquisition and communicative behaviour described in the previous chapter. If intervention is to be effective, we must gain an accurate and comprehensive picture of communicative behaviour. Observation should take account of:

- the frequency of communication (how often?);
- the range of contexts (different lessons? out of school?); and
- the similarities and differences between communication in school and at home.

From observation, we need to determine what learning stage the SLD child has reached. For example:

- is he making early gestures?
- is he producing single words?
- is he producing two or three word utterances? or
- is he attempting to use his language skills to communicate in different social situations?

The intervention programme will need to include both strands of learning; language content and communicative behaviour. It is important to reflect on the differences between children with communication difficulties who are assessed as SLD, and children with language disorders, or language delay, who may not have overall learning difficulties.

Working with the SLD child implies work on small-step targets; acceptance of a slow pace; reinforcement and revisiting; modelling of behaviours; repetition; and rewards for required responses. Chapter 8 contains practical suggestions for communication activities, which can be applied to SLD learners if they are broken down into manageable goals.

Language difficulties and IEPs

Children whose difficulties fall into any of the specialist categories described above will almost certainly have an intensive learning programme, based around their statement of SEN, which should be broken down into termly units of intervention, i.e. an IEP.

Many children with non-specialist language and communication problems may be on the school SEN register, as their difficulties in language and communication are highly likely to have resulted in some form of learning difficulty in reading, writing or numeracy.

Setting targets for IEPs

Targets represent learning goals, and identify what pupils will do, know or understand by the end of a stated time-scale. The strategies and resources on an IEP state what will be implemented to enable pupils to achieve their targets. Targets are more likely to be achieved if pupils are involved in learning goals wherever possible. Even pupils with SLD and poor communication can be involved to some degree.

A case study of target-setting for communication

Neil is Year 3 and has an SEN statement for severe/moderate learning difficulties. He also has language and communication difficulties. His targets set at last year's annual review have been achieved, and the targets for the next 12 months will be based on language and communicative behaviour. These will be broken down into goals for each term.

Communicative behaviour

- listen to peers when appropriate;
- share materials appropriately with peers (e.g. during literacy hour independent activities);
- listen attentively to adults for 15 minutes at a time;
- listen to, and follow instructions consistently;
- hand out resources to peers in the classroom;
- choose an appropriate time to speak; and
- give simple reason for a choice, e.g. the need for a blue crayon to colour the sky on a picture.

Language development:

- listen and respond to one-step instructions;
- speak in simple sentences – using basic adjectives and simple prepositions; and

- formulate own questions in relation to need, e.g. to visit the toilet, or to ask peers for a rubber.

Independence
- work independently of an adult for 10 minutes; and
- communicate with a range of people around school.

The school is to use a range of strategies and resources to help Neil achieve his targets. These include:
- opportunities for communication in different contexts and purposes, e.g. taking messages around school;
- focused work with the LSA daily; and
- goals to be 'written' in his book in picture form to remind Neil of what he is aiming towards.

Neil represents a range of children whose language and communicative development depend on a number of factors:
- opportunities to converse with a range of audiences for different purposes;
- clear targets for progression;
- pupil involvement in achieving own targets;
- a team approach, including parental support;
- effective role models for language and communication; and
- accurate, comprehensive and diagnostic assessment.

Bilingual learners

Children for whom English is an additional language (EAL) are not regarded as having SEN simply because they may experience difficulties in learning English. In order to identify bilingual learners with SEN, including language and communication difficulties, the difficulty must also be experienced in their mother tongue.

The majority of EAL children will not have SEN, but may experience initial difficulties brought about by the differences between e.g. Asian languages and English. Some of these differences are listed below to help teachers to understand the utterances produced by EAL pupils and to address their language needs.

Some differences between Urdu/Punjabi and English are as follows:

1. Word order — in English, the subject—verb—object structure, e.g. 'boy eating orange', in Asian languages could be 'boy orange eating'.
2. There is no definite article in Punjabi/Urdu.
3. Plurals — many Asian words have no plurals and may cause difficulties in English acquisition.
4. Questions — different intonation can turn a statement into a question.
5. Pronouns — there may be confusion in use of the third person singular in English, as regards gender.
6. Prepositions — in many Asian languages there are no prepositions, since the word to denote position is put after the noun, e.g. 'table under' instead of 'under the table'.
7. Asian speakers may also experience some difficulty in differentiating between letter sounds.

The list is intended only as an introduction to the kinds of difficulties which could arise. If in doubt, the specialist from the LEA bilingual service should be contacted.

This chapter has focused on a range of language and communication difficulties requiring general or specialist levels of intervention. These difficulties, combined with the stages of speaking and listening development explored in the previous chapter, provide the basic principles for a language and communication policy.

Chapter 4

A Policy for Language and Communication

Why do we need a policy for language and communication? Without a policy there is no common direction and therefore little consistency of teaching and learning throughout the school. If all children are to develop their language and communication skills from a child-centred perspective, continuity and progression derived from whole-school consistent policy is the essential foundation.

Philosophy

A policy for speaking and listening emanates from the beliefs of professionals who teach these skills. Since English is the medium for curriculum delivery, part of the philosophy may be that all teachers are responsible for developing language and literacy, whatever their subject. If staff as a whole believe that speaking and listening form the foundations of all learning, school policy reflects that belief. A policy which achieves whole-school consensus is more likely to result in consistent practice.

Policy aim and objectives

What does a policy for language and communication aim to achieve? Staff who accept the philosophical statements above may aim to raise speaking and listening standards for all pupils and enable maximum cross-curricular learning potential.

Objectives

What objectives would facilitate the stated aim/s? These aims could be to:

- improve the language skills of all children;
- develop the communicative behaviour of all children;
- recognise all pupils' learning potential and build on this;
- assess speaking and listening skills more effectively; and
- involve all staff in the development of speaking and listening.

Policy principles

The strength of a policy rests on its principles. These are the foundations on which to build procedures of what is to be done and how. The following areas may stimulate useful debate on the principles underpinning a policy of speaking and listening for all.

1. Activities for speaking and listening should reflect their interrelationship with reading and writing, and recognise that each enriches the development of the others.
2. Activities for developing language and communication should be based on exciting and interesting multi-sensory approaches.
3. Listening and speaking activities should include real purposes and audiences.
4. Intervention programmes for language and communication should be informed by comprehensive assessment of a child's skills. Teaching should build on children's strengths in order to move them forward.
5. Communication should include signing where necessary.

6. Speaking and listening should extend to form a cross-curricular network of balanced activities.
7. All staff share responsibility for speaking and listening.
8. The policy will be supported by an effective staff development programme.
9. The policy builds on the strengths of existing procedures for teaching language and communication.
10. The speaking and listening policy reflects the needs of every pupil in the school.
11. The teaching of standard English respects the differences of other languages, dialects and accents.
12. The involvement of parents is essential to pupils' language and communication development.
13. The policy takes due account of gender, recognising different learning needs and styles.

The extent to which the above principles are accepted will determine the procedures which are to reflect them.

Policy procedure

The policy should also state what the school does to achieve its aims and objectives, and to reflect its principles.

Department for Education and Employment (DfEE) requirements

The policy needs to clarify for all staff how national requirements are to be incorporated into it, for example:

- the National Curriculum requirements of range, key skills, and standard English and language study;
- the National Literacy Strategy (NLS) – how do speaking and listening support the development of reading and writing? and
- the National Numeracy Strategy – how does the speaking and listening curriculum link in with and support maths?

Opportunities for speaking and listening

To maintain continuity and progression, the policy could further identify the opportunities offered for all children to develop their speaking and listening skills. For example:

- a range of focused group work – in pairs, small and larger groups, pupils and teacher, grouping arrangements which mix different classes and so on;
- interactive talk across the curriculum, e.g. how are speaking and listening in subject areas used to enhance both language and communication development as well as subject learning? Chapter 6 develops this area;
- real audiences – who are they? Do they include visiting authors for children to listen to and question about their books and a range of people around the school and in the community, where safe and appropriate?
- genuine purposes – how genuine is the talk that takes place? Does it aim to find out real information, for example surveys and interviews?

Coverage of language areas identified

Staff may wish to ensure a shared understanding, through the policy, of how the areas of language identified in Chapter 2 are to be developed as tools for communication. For example, the language of school and the environment;

reading and book awareness; language of writing; language of maths; vocabulary of reading schemes; cross-curricular words; main vocabulary of stories read to children; and language of games and group work.

Independence and communicative behaviour

What approaches and methods are used throughout the school to develop strategies for speaking and listening, and which activities will feature? For example, will positive communicative behaviour be modelled? Will pupils have opportunities to practice the behaviour required within an atmosphere of sensitive guidance, e.g. turn-taking? How is independence developed as part of communication?

Use of in-school support staff

How do LSAs support the policy for speaking and listening? Do they work in the literacy hour, on focused language work with groups, individuals, or both? What about SEN specialist teachers and advisers? How are they included as human resources for the development of language and communication?

Resources

The policy should state the resources available and where they are stored, and could include suggestions for their use. Are resources stored in a central area, or are they kept separately in classrooms?

Roles and responsibilities

These form a key section of any policy. Who has overall responsibility for the implementation of the language and communication procedures? How are staff consulted? How is consensus gained? How is consistency ensured?

Staff development

It is important to consider who is to plan and deliver the training to all staff involved in language and communication. How is the literacy coordinator involved, and the school special educational needs coordinator (SENCO)? What basic skills and knowledge does the policy require all staff to have, or to acquire? Does the policy aim to have at least one teacher with an award-bearing qualification in language? Who undertakes the training of class teachers; LSA staff; parents or volunteers?

Equal opportunities

How are all cultures and minority groups allowed equal opportunities to progress? How is entitlement to the literacy hour facilitated for all pupils? What differentiation strategies are used? This section of the policy may state how the needs of bilingual learners and the range of SEN pupils are assessed and provided for.

Assessment and recording

How are speaking and listening skills assessed? Where is the evidence taken from? How are pupils' language skills and strategies recorded on a continuous, cumulative and summative basis? Chapter 10 develops this area.

Parental involvement

Parents play a key role in any policy for children's learning. The language policy may state how parents are to be involved in language development. Do parents share the responsibility for language and communication skills? If so, how? Research has proved that home and school links are crucial to all children's learning. If the value of parental support is to be maximised, procedures need to be consistent. Are parents used in the classroom during the literacy hour? Are they sometimes part of interactive group talk?

Links with other policies

The language and communication policy should link in and be consistent with policies for: assessment; parental involvement; SEN policy; literacy plan; curricular policies; staff development; and resources.

Evaluation of the policy

What performance indicators are used to determine the effectiveness of the policy? These could include:

- improved levels of pupils' speaking and listening;
- raised standards of cross-curricular learning;
- improved confidence of staff; and
- improved liaison between internal staff and external support agencies.

To identify improved levels of speaking and listening, it is necessary to know what they were at the starting point.

Where do we start?

First tasks could be to brainstorm the philosophy, aim and objectives and principles held by all staff. Whole-school discussion could highlight views and opinions which have never been aired, and invite a completely fresh approach to language and communication in the school, in the light of current DfEE initiatives.

A thorough audit of practice will help to collate information on what is currently done. The above questions may be helpful in providing section headings for audit. The process of clarifying and evaluating current practice as part of policy review also acts as an ongoing staff development exercise for the benefit of language and communication in the school.

This chapter has raised many questions, and provided few answers, as the success of any policy depends on the collective decision-making of the professionals who devise it. Many of the issues raised here are explored in further chapters.

Chapter 5

Talk in the Literacy Hour

Speaking and listening are scarcely mentioned in the *National Literacy Strategy: Framework for Teaching*, yet they are woven through the fabric of its objectives. The role of speaking and listening appears briefly in the introduction:

> Literacy unites the important skills of reading and writing. It also involves speaking and listening, which although they are not separately identified in the framework, are an essential part of it. Good oral work enhances pupils' understanding of language in both oral and written forms and of the way language can be used to communicate. It is also an important part of the process through which pupils read and compose texts. (DfEE 1998b.)

The daily literacy hour is the pivot around which the NLS revolves.

During a recent workshop session, a group of primary teachers expressed concern that speaking and listening skills are not identified as part of the Framework, feeling that if oracy is so crucial to learning, its development should be part of the package. Yet, from a practical perspective, could schools possibly cope with a sequence of objectives for speaking and listening alongside those for reading and writing? The author believes not.

Speaking and listening are not really absent from the NLS Framework; their invisible threads bind the NLS together. As the objectives for reading and writing are planned, their delivery, through talk, brings into focus the approaches and methods which are meant to hold all children, including the majority of those with SEN, into the brisk pace of teaching and learning.

Figure 5.1 models the tenuous relationship between the learner and his desired goals. Language skills and communicative behaviour separate the two, acting as enabling factors or barriers, depending on whether a child's levels of speaking and listening are effectively developed or not.

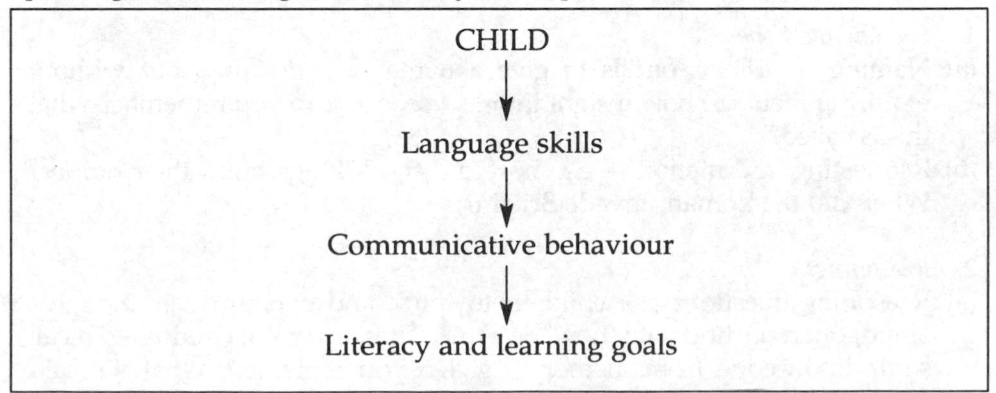

Figure 5.1 Language and communication – enabler or barrier?

Working with children who have underdeveloped language and communication can make it difficult for teachers to establish talk as the central link to learning. If the literacy hour is to focus on identified reading and writing objectives, then within that hour teachers can only address speaking and listening difficulties, and ensure all children are engaging with the activities, through appropriate differentiation.

Children with an IEP for language and communication need additional, focused time with a skilled adult to address their targets outside of the literacy hour. This chapter explores speaking and listening through the literacy hour, while further chapters consider focused intervention and practical activities elsewhere in the curriculum.

Whole-class talk in the literacy hour

The literacy hour encourages a move away from working with individuals to working with the class as a whole, and with groups. Schools adopting the hour will spend two thirds of it on whole-class teaching, through speaking and listening. It is worth reflecting on how all children can benefit.

Children with SEN should benefit from whole-class teaching provided that they can access it; care needs to be taken that all children are included. There may be a tendency to focus on those who present the greatest challenges, e.g. behaviour difficulties, while children who make little fuss are not included within the whole class dialogue. Children who rarely join in oral work need to be drawn into the joint speaking and listening.

Shared text work uses language to enhance reading and writing, but can develop language skills effectively at the same time. The focus of text discussion is on exploring and extending understanding through carefully-directed questioning and sensitive responses. Whole-class work offers all children a chance to strengthen their overall awareness of books and book language.

Differentiated questioning

Whole-class work relies on differentiated questioning: if all children are to benefit from the interaction, with their interest held for a full half-hour, it is worth exploring the techniques of questioning. The basic idea is that all children are asked questions which invite a response dependent upon their capability, yet which allows them to demonstrate what they know, and to experience success through oral interaction.

Barnes *et al.* (1971) well-respected research and analysis of classroom language has renewed significance for the literacy hour. Barnes studied the kinds of questions asked by teachers in Year 7 classrooms, but the points made apply to classroom language at any key stage. Barnes identified different kinds of questions:

1. *Factual questions*

(a) Naming – asking pupils to give a name to something, but without requiring them to show insight into its use, e.g. 'can you remember what this is called?'

(b) Requesting information – e.g. how did the Vikings build their homes? When did the Romans invade Britain?

2. *Reasoning*

(a) Reasoning questions ask children to think and express their thoughts aloud, often starting with 'how' or 'why'. These may ask children to recall some knowledge from memory, e.g. Do you remember what we said yesterday about . . . ? Reasoning questions can be 'open', and allow the response to be whatever the listener (child) wants it to be, or 'closed', requiring only one correct answer.

(b) Observation questions require the child to look at something and interpret what he is seeing. For example, when introducing a text, a teacher may ask pupils to look at the front cover, and ask them to interpret it: 'what do you think the cover is telling us?' 'What kind of book is this?'

3. Open questions do not have to require reasoning, e.g. 'Who can give me the name of a famous author?' They are open in the sense that a child can offer any author as a correct response, yet questions do not rely on reasoning, only memory and knowledge.

4. *Social questions*
(a) Control questions seek to impose a teacher's wishes upon the class, e.g. 'Let's write about . . . , shall we?'
(b) Appeal questions may ask pupils to agree or to share an attitude, and are easier for pupils to disagree with.

As part of their research, Barnes *et al.* (1971) also observed that few questions were asked because the teacher needed to know the answer. The implications for today's classrooms, particularly during the literacy hour, are clear.

Consider the following questions. Into which category could they fall, and how does knowing about different kinds of questions help us to engage all children during whole class work?

- What did the jigaree do? (Answer – he jumped or danced)
- What would your jigaree do? (more open?)
- Why did we stop at the end of this word?
- Where do you think we should start writing?
- How would you say that?
- What can you see at the top of this page?
- Where shall I put my full stop?
- Can you think of another word for this?
- Can you think of a better way to write this?
- Which word do you prefer?
- Are you going to redraft your story now?

Clearly, some questions are more enabling than others, and actively encourage learners to project their thinking. Only by knowing different children's language and communication skills can teachers differentiate class-based questions.

The purpose of questions

The purpose of a question and the child to whom it is directed may determine the type of question asked, the vocabulary used, and the scope allowed for the response. Teachers may differentiate the language used in a question by:

- reducing the number of words used;
- intonation, e.g. stressing the meaning-carrying words;
- deliberately avoiding abstract language to retain clarity; and
- stressing the question word itself – who, how, what – to cue a child into the response required.

Questions do not have to be directed, but need to be clear enough for all children to offer a response. If aimed at particular children, the level of language needs to reflect the child's progress on the developmental scale. For a child with a semantic–pragmatic language disorder then the words will be chosen to aid the listener's understanding, and time will be allowed for a response. A visual aid will help understanding.

If the question is directed at a language-disadvantaged child whose IEP target is to respond and to use simple sentences, then the question will not be too complex and the main words to be understood and responded to will be stressed. This technique requires far more than simplifying vocabulary, and speaking at an appropriate pace. Asking a question sends a child's thoughts into a particular direction: closed questioning may limit reasoning, while open questions can offer the child scope to extend their reasoning.

The purpose of the question also determines its format and precision. Is the question aiming to:

- open up discussion in a general sense?
- guide children's thoughts into a particular direction?
- engage the interest of one child, or the class by personalising it: 'What would your jigaree do?' or
- test understanding of a particular concept?

If class discussion is to engage all children, differentiated questioning strategies are crucial.

Focused word and sentence work

Talking about words and their meanings is central to the communicative process. Two quotations from the writings of Lewis Carroll (1962a, b), Figure 5.2, illustrate the point about words and their meanings, particularly homonyms, and the potential difficulties for children whose vocabulary and understanding are underdeveloped.

1. Extract from *Through the Looking-Glass*
'How is bread made?'
'I know *that*! ' Alice cried eagerly. 'You take some flour—'
' Where do you pick the flower?' the White Queen asked, 'In a garden, or in the hedges?'
'Well, it isn't *picked* at all, 'Alice explained: 'it's *ground*— '
'How many acres of ground?' said the White Queen.

2. Extract from *Alice's Adventures in Wonderland*
'Mine is a long and a sad tale!' said the Mouse, turning to Alice and sighing.
'It is a long tail certainly,' said Alice, looking down with wonder at the Mouse's tail; 'but why do you call it sad?'

Figure 5.2 Words and their meanings, from Carroll (1962a, b)

Homonymous relations are widespread in English and are the source of confusion for many children. Yet, as vocabulary develops, and children begin to appreciate language and its potential, they can also be a source of delight.

Vocabulary development

From the reception stage, as part of the NLS focus on vocabulary, children are to collect new and significant words, the aim being to extend their repertoire of language. The Carroll extracts stress the importance of identifying words in their context. Consider the following examples:

Gear: I need some new gear (clothes) for the party.
The gears need attention. (to the garage mechanic)
Soft: This jumper feels lovely and soft.
Don't be so soft!
He sounds a bit soft in the head.

Vocabulary development as part of the literacy hour has the potential to extend basic concepts and vocabulary, as well as to enrich children's choices and overall appropriateness of words. All children must understand what is presented at text level so that they can fully respond at word level, so that their vocabulary suggestions reflect the right context.

Word work

The NLS Framework requires, 'systematic and frequent teaching of phonological awareness, phonics and spelling throughout Key Stage 1.' The medium of teaching all these skills is talk. This part of the hour should help all children to develop their skills, provided they can access the delivery.

Phonological awareness does not follow a sequence, unlike phonics. The ability to recognise differences in the sounds of letters, letter strings or syllables can be developed by using any grouped vocabulary from the text. Phonological awareness precedes reading, so that children are aware of the syllables in 'hippopotamus' and 'cat' before they read the words, yet it also develops out of learning to read. Children at all levels of language development benefit from the experiences, but the points made in Chapter 3 concerning sensory impaired children need to be noted.

Talk about phonics and spelling in the literacy hour needs careful differentiation depending upon the range of skills children have. The objectives in the NLS Framework need to be adhered to as far as possible, but without overloading the capacity of particular children to learn from the experience.

For example, if the 'ee' sound is the focus of discussion, yet triple consonant clusters are a problem for certain children, the word 'screech' may cause overload. If children have been working on single syllable words, e.g. cat, pot, hip, as part of their individual phonic programme, then keep, peel, been are easier for the child than 'screech', as the 'ee' sound has no interference from the doubling or tripling of the consonants. Children with articulation difficulties will be helped by word work, provided that their imperfect responses are sensitively received.

The Framework states that decoding skills should be, 'taught through carefully structured activities which help pupils to hear and discriminate regularities in speech, and to see how these are related to letters and letter combinations in reading and spelling.'

Grammatical awareness

As grammatical awareness features strongly as part of the literacy hour, we need to clarify what grammar is. Bunting (1997) describes grammar as, 'the system of rules by which parts of words, words and sentences combine and relate to make meaning.' Bunting also refers to three distinct, yet interrelated elements of grammar:

- syntax – the structural relations of words and parts of words;
- phonology – the study of the sounds of a language; and
- semantics – the study of the meanings of words and sentences.

The grammar element of the literacy hour is an opportunity for children with language disadvantages to develop their targets through the NLS objectives. Awareness of the basic language levels of children should help teachers to pitch general grammar work at a level which enables all children to respond; for example, work on capital letters and full stops may use different levels of sentences as practice material, and include other punctuation elements for more able children.

The NLS objectives for sentence work partly focus on the function of words in different sentences and contexts. Consider the word 'green' in the following sentences:

> Pat was wearing a green dress.
> Due to heavy rain, the green was waterlogged.
> The office boy was still a bit green.

For children with language difficulties, where vocabulary and understanding are underdeveloped, focusing on the use of words in their context will help children to: see that the same words can have different meanings; understand that meaning (oral and written) derives from sentences within the text; and regard complete sentences as units of meaning which should make sense.

Sensory impaired children in the literacy hour

Access issues for children with hearing and visual impairments are similar to those for children with language and communication difficulties.

Hearing impaired (HI) children

During the whole-class input, HI children will need to:

- see the teacher's face and lips;
- have vocabulary work reinforced with pictures or real objects as visual aids;
- have the responses of other pupils repeated, especially if peers are not facing the HI child; and
- have a clear view of the teacher and the text, which should be away from the window if possible to prevent shadow.

All of us tend to use gestures, some of which are helpful, e.g. facial expressions which help to convey meaning to the HI or language-disadvantaged child. It may be difficult to remember not to cover our mouths with our hands, or talk as we write on the board without turning to face the class, but simple points such as these can enhance access for all children, not only the HI pupils.

Visually impaired (VI) children

Children with visual impairment are helped by sitting at the front and encouraged to actively listen. Blind children will need Braille copies of the text, and/or the main meaning-carrying words to help them cue in to the shared reading. Partially-sighted children should also be seated at the front. Access is helped by a text with good contrast and bold print. Speaking while writing on the whiteboard helps the partially-sighted child to follow what is going on.

It is also helpful to state what is being looked at during the shared reading or word work, e.g. pictures. Pointing alone does not help the partially-sighted pupil. It is easy to overlook the need to verbalise, e.g. by describing the illustrations in a big book, but Braille does not compensate for colourful pictures which enhance the text. Saying children's names will help VI children to know who is responding to questions. Raised eyebrows or pursed lips have little effect on the VI child, or any child who does not recognise details of facial expression.

Children with severe learning difficulties (SLD)

Many of the strategies suggested above can also help SLD children to focus on whole-class input more easily. A picture really is worth a thousand words if it enables less able children to absorb a point of discussion, or to understand and remember a new word.

Group talk in the literacy hour

The majority of children with language and communication difficulties will be helped to develop their skills through group work. Groups may be:

- formed for a range of purposes, possibly with different tasks to perform;
- of varying sizes – pairs, threes or table-size; and
- constant or fluid, depending on the reasons for their existence, e.g. ability groups may change members over time as children progress at

different rates, and friendship groups change frequently as friends fall out with each other.

In the literacy hour, and at other times, groups need to achieve maximum performance and operate independently, whatever the task. The effectiveness of group work depends on all members of the group: understanding what they have to do; respecting other members of the group; and communicating with peers in the group.

Consider the following examples of IEP targets for communicative behaviour. How could the focus of group work help pupils to:

- express personal needs to peers, e.g. request a rubber?
- listen to the requests of others, and respond appropriately?
- share in the joint use of group equipment and tools?
- listen and speak respectfully during group discussion?
- respect the personal space of other children, e.g. when children are sharing a desk? or
- provide fair, constructive criticism of others' writing?

Group work will help children to achieve the above targets, and others of a similar nature. Individual targets for communicative behaviour could be written into children's books as reminders of their goals or, if joint targets, could be displayed in a prominent place for all children to observe. Figure 5.3 illustrates joint goals for communicating as part of a group.

To be a good member of a group:

1. Listen to what others say – think about it.
2. Wait for a pause before you speak – think about your words.
3. When taking turns, watch others and be ready when your turn comes round.
4. Be polite. Say what you think with respect for others.
5. Share things you all need for a task and look after group equipment.

Figure 5.3 How to be a good member of a group

Guided reading and writing

During guided reading or writing, while the focus remains firmly on literacy objectives, the oral element of the work can be more specifically directed. When working with ability groups:

- new vocabulary from the shared text can be reinforced;
- NLS objectives can be matched to pupils' IEP targets more directly; and
- each pupil's language and communication difficulties can be taken account of, enhancing the overall effectiveness of guided reading and writing as well as the oral work.

Guided reading and writing enables teachers to move all elements of language forward, and offers more focused opportunities to assess language and communication through children's responses.

Developing independence

The literacy hour relies on children working independently for 20 minutes. Working independently does not always mean working alone, but implies being able to remain on task, change activities, seek help, find information, work with different groups and so on, without an adult.

All children need to know exactly what is meant by independence if they are to achieve it. Children with language and communication difficulties need to know where they are, and precisely how to behave, during an independent activity. They may need:

- additional reinforcement of the task;
- a picture or object which cues them in to the task; or
- a reminder that they are working without the teacher, e.g. a teddy on the work table for younger children, or a notice for older ones (with a picture for less able readers).

Enabling all children to work independently, and to develop independent language and literacy skills, is a difficult and time-consuming, but highly rewarding, task. For children who find it difficult even to ask for a ruler, try: writing key phrases or sentences on card (see examples in Figure 5.4), with a picture if necessary, to start them off and give them confidence; or talking to groups about patience and understanding of different needs. Encourage effective language users to support the needs of others through positive responses and sensitive language prompts where necessary. Peer support can be of considerable benefit to the child with language and communication difficulties.

May I have a pencil, please?	I need a . . . please.
I don't know what to do.	May I go to the toilet?
Which page are we up to?	What do I need to do next?
Where can I find . . . ?	Who am I working with?
Which group am I working with?	

Figure 5.4 Key sentences for independence

Plenary

Children with speaking and listening difficulties will benefit from revisiting and consolidating their work, and communicating this to the class, even if they only say a few words. Opportunities to summarise and review what has been done helps to reinforce the learning process for all pupils, especially those with learning difficulties.

Consider the following target areas, and how the plenary section of the literacy hour could contribute to a child's achievement of them. Communication targets could include:

- exhibiting own work, and explaining it to the class (targeting confidence);
- remembering what has been done in the lesson and talking about it (targeting memory skills); and
- stating what has been learned in the lesson (targeting own involvement in learning as a key part of communication).

The literacy hour has the potential to take children anywhere. Texts which portray different cultures will open up new worlds for many pupils. Delicate issues such as bereavement, drugs, war or racism can all emerge as talking points, depending on the texts used. This is all to the good as long as children with language difficulties are helped to fully understand the concepts presented, and have further opportunities, possibly with an LSA, to reinforce the new vocabulary as necessary.

The literacy hour has the power to enhance language skills and communication for all children, provided that it is sensitively and creatively taught. The rigorous skill-based approach to literacy needs to take account of language in its whole context, and be transferred into lively and meaningful cross-curricular learning.

Chapter 6

Communication Across the Curriculum

The NLS Framework

> covers the statutory requirements for reading and writing in the National Curriculum for English and contributes substantially to the development of speaking and listening. It is also relevant to teaching across the whole of the National Curriculum. Skills, especially those that focus on reading and writing non-fiction texts, should be linked to and applied in every subject. (Introduction to the *NLS: Framework for Teaching;* DfEE 1998b.)

This chapter explores language and communication through the curriculum.

Cross-curricular talk

The National Curriculum provides the content for school-based learning and states the key skills and knowledge which subscribe to it. The NLS and, from September 1999, the National Numeracy Strategy (NNS), provides structured areas of experience through which school-based learning happens. Across the curriculum, learning is the acquisition of new knowledge.

Information does not automatically become knowledge. Those who swotted for GCE examinations may recall hours spent 'learning' voluminous information in order to regurgitate it and gain a GCE in that particular subject. Knowledge appeared simply as what could be stored in the memory, understood or not. In many cases, much of it was not understood but, during that era, lessons rarely encouraged talk.

Talk turns information into knowledge by helping us to make sense of the new information with which we are bombarded every day. A brief note between colleagues, often needing clarification or further details, is an example of this new information. Those who have worked with the so-called integrated day, or through cross-curricular topics, may lament the way in which the National Curriculum has separated subject information unnaturally into compartments without encouraging their integration as knowledge. The following sections explore cross-curricular talk at each stage of learning.

Talk in the early years

The possible introduction of children under five to Key Stage 1 of the National Curriculum has highlighted for early years teachers the dangers of introducing young children to discrete subject areas too soon.

In one sense, all of early years education is cross-curricular, and the desirable outcomes for learning are intended to represent the integrated knowledge of early years children in the six areas of learning. The following extracts from the desirable outcome for 'knowledge and understanding of the world' show what children should be able to do as they enter compulsory education. Children should be able to:

- talk about where they live . . . environment . . . families, and past and present events in their own lives;
- explore and recognise features of living things, objects and events in the natural and man-made world;
- talk about their observations, sometimes recording them;

- ask questions to gain information about why things happen and how things work;
- explore and select materials and equipment, and use skills such as cutting, joining and folding for a variety of purposes; and
- use technology where appropriate to support their learning.

The above outcomes provide a foundation for historical, geographical, scientific and technological learning. Consider extracts for creative development, which require children to:

- explore sound and colour, texture, shape, form and space;
- respond in a variety of ways to what they see, hear, smell, touch and feel;
- show increasing ability to use imagination, to listen and to observe, through art, music, dance and imaginative play; and
- use a widening range of materials, suitable tools, instruments and other resources to express ideas and communicate their feelings.

The early years offers children opportunities for talk that is specifically geared towards the National Curriculum, and should enable the majority to access the Key Stage 1 subject curriculum on entry.

Implications for children with communication problems

The early years presents the first and best opportunity to observe all children as individuals in their learning environment. The desirable outcomes offer guidance and direction to early years establishments and should enable staff to:

- assess what individual children bring to their learning environment, i.e. their strengths and weaknesses;
- identify children with learning difficulties who may need specialist support, e.g. speech and language therapy, and refer the child for further specialist assessment;
- identify children with underdeveloped language and communication skills and implement individual programmes to address them;
- start to involve children in their own learning, and begin to operate an independence training programme; and
- inform parents of language and communication difficulties and involve them in their child's intervention programme.

Early learning develops through play and talk, and needs to be focused towards the next stage of learning, yet take account of individual capacities as children move forward.

National Curriculum at Key Stage 1

The following statement is found on page 1 of each National Curriculum document (DfE 1995a, b, c). 'Pupils should be taught to express themselves clearly in speech and writing and to develop their reading skills.' The clear message is that English is to be developed through the National Curriculum.
Consider the statement from Key Stage 1 history programmes of study (DfE 1995c). 'Pupils should be given opportunities to develop an awareness of the past and . . . ways in which it is different from the present. They should be helped . . . to understand . . . ways in which we find out about the past.'
From *Geography in the National Curriculum* (DfE 1995b), 'a) investigate the physical and human features of their surroundings, and b) undertake studies that focus on geographical questions, e.g. What/where is it? What is it like? How did it get like this?' Talk is at the core of the National Curriculum programmes of study.

Cross-curricular opportunities at Key Stage 1 stem from investigative and collaborative activities in pairs and groups and should incorporate a smooth transition from play-based to more formal learning. Only when children have thoroughly explored the language and concepts described in the desirable outcomes are they ready to extend their cross-curricular experiences into more defined areas of learning.

Bilingual children will benefit from collaborative activities with English-speaking peers. Real objects and stimulating equipment provide the focus for more explicit speaking and listening activities, through which children can draw on different language forms and extend their vocabulary in different curricular contexts.

To benefit from the NLS objectives for Key Stage 1, children need to talk about aspects of language as part of their reading and writing activities. In so doing, they are thinking consciously about the language they use. For example, in Year 1, they will use their spoken language to:

- check that written language makes sense;
- draw on grammatical awareness . . . to read with appropriate expression and intonation;
- notice the difference between spoken and written forms;
- explore and play with rhyming patterns; and
- collect new or significant words.

For all children, especially those with language and communication difficulties, thinking consciously about language needs to be a cross-curricular activity. The process of building historical, scientific, technological or artistic vocabulary stems from conscious thought about particular words, and how they are used in that subject.

Talk at Key Stage 2

Opportunities and experiences through Key Stage 2 will build on those encountered in the earlier years. The process for developing speaking and listening will be similar to what has gone before, but children should be learning to use spoken language with increasing control and precision. Cross-curricular vocabulary should reflect a more sophisticated use of nouns and verbs specific to the subject. For example, in science, a paper clip will be described as 'attracted' to a magnet, rather than merely 'sticking to it'.

Children should be using language to reflect on what they have learned, e.g. to analyse, select, consider or evaluate, through the thought processes of 'how' and 'why.' For example:

- why did the Roman civilisation end?
- why did the liquid turn yellow?
- how are motorway bridges built?
- how can we talk to someone in America?

Subject talk in the secondary school

The transition to secondary school can highlight problems for children with language and communication difficulties unless appropriate support is provided. The many differences between primary and secondary education include:

- a range of teachers, and variations in language styles;
- variations in the kind of communicative behaviour expected, e.g. talking with peers may be accepted in one lesson, but not in another;
- a more defined use of subject vocabulary;
- the need to work more often with different peer groups;
- the need for a child to find his own way around a large school; and
- the impersonal atmosphere of a large building, with possibly over 1000 pupils and many different teachers, who may not know all pupils by name for a while, and who are often supplemented by temporary staff.

Social adequacy depends on being articulate. Consider the problems faced by children:

- needing the security of routine and familiarity, e.g. children with some form of autistic spectrum disorder;
- learning English as a second language who have not yet learned to formulate questions in English;
- with speech impediments;
- whose thinking is limited, e.g. those with a moderate learning difficulty (MLD);
- who are still learning to converse in simple sentences, e.g. with SLD;
- who communicate by signing;
- who cannot understand and process what is said with enough speed to record lesson notes, or their homework; and
- whose vocabulary is still limited.

Suggestions for speaking and listening activities

The following activities can be adapted for any age group, and will help to address the problems listed above as part of a general, class-based approach to developing language and communication through subject experience. According to their abilities, children could:

- make a class book of historical, geographical words etc., with pictures to support less able children;
- choose a subject word (word or picture on card picked out of an envelope) and talk about it for two or three minutes at the end of a lesson;
- play pair and group games with core subject vocabulary
- interview a range of people, e.g. peers, head teacher, lollipop lady, caretaker; and
- do problem-solving or decision-making activities, e.g. what shall we do about this donation for our funds/the vandalism around the school? and so on.

Developing subject vocabulary

Many difficulties faced by less able communicators can be eased by the specific teaching of subject vocabulary. This will support all pupils and teachers by:

- improving knowledge and understanding of the subject;
- enhancing enjoyment of the subject through improved knowledge of the vocabulary used;
- promoting confidence for the whole range of pupils; and
- contributing to the development of language *per se*.

The Lewis Carroll extracts in Figure 5.2 illustrate how vocabulary is easily misunderstood; yet to teach all of the subject words would be time-consuming and counter-productive to the learning process. What is the core subject vocabulary through which the subject is delivered, and therefore necessary for the learner to understand it? Which of the subject words listed in Figure 6.1 would appear on your core list, as vocabulary to be specifically taught?

Maths	Geography	History	Art	Music
circle	climate	source	artist	composer
shape	extinct	bias	colour	orchestra
multiply	relief	evidence	palette	rhythm
divide	glacial	feudal	primary	performance
equal	afforested	revolution	technique	tempo

Figure 6.1 Subject vocabulary

Common and specific subject vocabulary

How much of the vocabulary in Figure 6.1 is specific to the subject itself, and how much of it is used in a subject-specific way? Consider the following examples:

Circle: Draw a circle with a radius of 6 cm.
Place your chairs in a circle.
Golf clubs often have social circles.

Divide: Divide into groups of three or four.
How do we divide twelve by six?
The class divide is exemplified by the social circles to which people belong.

Barnes *et al.* (1971) suggest that the desire to teach the terminology of the subject, as exemplified by Figure 6.2, may impede communication, particularly for less able pupils. The example illustrates the focus on naming, at the possible expense of understanding, the processes and functions of the biological topic discussed.

T: Where does it go then?
P: To your lungs, Miss.
T: Where does it go before it reaches your lungs? . . . Paul.
P: Your windpipe, Miss.
T: Down the windpipe . . . Now can anyone remember the other word for windpipe?
P: The trachea.
T: The trachea . . . good . . . After it has gone through the trachea, where does it go then? . . . There are a lot of little pipes going into the lungs . . .What are those called? . . . Ian?
P: The bronchii.
T: The bronchii . . . that's the plural. What's the singular? What is one of these tubes called? . . . Ann.
P: Bronchus.
T: Bronchus . . . with 'us' at the end . . . What does 'inspiration' mean?

Figure 6.2 Subject language in the classroom, from *Language, the Learner and the School* (Barnes *et al.* 1971)

This is an example of specialist language delivered to pupils in a deliberate way, the purpose being to teach terminology specific to the subject, and used only for that purpose. A major reason why many pupils fail to access science is its reliance on specialist and technical terminology.

There is a further important point to this discussion of subject language. Barnes *et al.* (1971) also suggested that teachers often operate within the register of their particular subject. If pupils fail to answer a question, or do not use that register through their explanation, the teacher fails to see that a pupil has understood the concept, but has simply responded in his own more familiar language register. This may have implications for how teachers judge responses to oral work. Observing pupils' appropriate use of subject vocabulary is a necessary aim. Yet, learners must understand vocabulary before they can produce it. Pupils may demonstrate their understanding of vocabulary, through their own words, before they produce the specific subject vocabulary.

Finally, consider the way in which pupils may receive instructions, e.g. 'observe this'. The word 'observe' is a common instruction and can be delivered by teachers in any number of ways. For children with underdeveloped language, which instruction would achieve the most effective response?

- 'What do you observe about this substance?' or
- 'Observe the substance and watch the colour change. Write down the new colour.'

The exploration of questions in Chapter 5 suggested that closed questioning may inhibit some pupils and limit their responses. Conversely, instructions which are too open fail to focus attention on the point of the exercise. Instructions for less able pupils, especially those with SLD, are more likely to achieve an outcome when they are precise and carefully structured.

Enhancing access to subject vocabulary

1. Start by knowing which words are the priority for learning. Some pupils may not be able to learn all the words. Which ones should they focus on?
2. Have groups of pupils compile subject dictionaries, each group working on a section of the alphabet, as shown in Figure 6.3. The discussion of meanings to compile the word dictionary, followed by the discussion of different groups in editing the dictionary, will result in a valuable exploration of the meaning of subject words. Such activities can cross-over into the literacy hour at any level, e.g. into work on the alphabet and dictionary objectives.
3. When speaking, place stress on the word to be learned and help children to focus their attention on it. Include a picture or object where possible to help them remember the new word.
4. Pupils could take turns to talk about the word for a few minutes or, alternatively, could find pictures to match the word, cut out from old textbooks kept for the purpose.
5. Pupils could work in groups to put subject words in sentences, reinforcing each child's conceptual understanding.
6. Have pupils mime the subject words being learned for a few minutes at the end of a lesson. Pupils have to guess the right word from the mime. This will help to reinforce new words, and help train pupils to respond to gesture.
7. Use the phonic element of the new words to help them remember it, e.g. play 'hangman' games.
8. Categorise the new words with others, e.g. food words, Roman words, Viking words, clothes words.
9. As subject words are being discussed, link them with reading and writing. Once a word has been taught, and is understood, seeing it on a piece of card, or as a wall display, will aid pupils' memories.
10. Use rhyme, where it naturally occurs, to help pupils remember subject vocabulary.

Talking about subject vocabulary

Research has shown that children's talk during group work is inhibited when a teacher is present. When a teacher or adult is not part of the interaction, as an authoritative figure, children are free to discuss on a more equal level, and use language differently. Predictably, many show greater assertiveness, and use counter-argument. The exchanges may not be as neatly presented as in teacher-directed discussion, and may, where positive communicative behaviour is undeveloped, come to a halt for lack of the teacher or adult as arbiter. Nevertheless, group discussion without an adult, but with a clear task outcome, is one way in which children with poor language and communication can practise their skills with peers.

TASK BOARD

Task: Making a subject dictionary for science

1. Take out from our subject list the words for your group.
2. List your group words in alphabetical order.
3. Write meanings for your group words:

Group	Task
Circles	letters A to E
Squares	letters F to J
Triangles	letters K to O
Rectangles	letters P to T
Ovals	letters U to Z

For next session:

1. Groups share their meanings with one other group.
2. Each group redrafts its work.
3. The complete dictionary is word-processed on the computer.
4. Copies are prepared for the reference area.

Figure 6.3 Making a subject dictionary

The following sections focus on areas of the curriculum, where speaking and listening play a dominant and valuable role, or present significant issues to be dealt with.

Talk in English

The NLS provides the philosophy and structure for raising achievement in English for all pupils up to Year 6. While the literacy hour plays a major role at primary level, other areas of English, namely drama and literature, complement what takes place in the literacy hour, and form an important element of English at every key stage.

Role of drama

Drama is a development of the 'let's pretend' play of early years. *English in the National Curriculum* (DfE 1995a) at Key Stage 1 states that, 'Pupils should be encouraged to participate in drama activities, improvisation and performances of various kinds, using language appropriate to a role or situation'. At Key Stage 2, pupils should, 'participate in a wide range of drama activities, including improvisation, role-play, and the writing and performance of scripted drama.'

What role does drama play in the curriculum, and how can it help to address language and communication difficulties? Drama offers a framework and a methodology for spoken language, and provides scope for pupils to explore social, moral, domestic and historical ideas and attitudes.

Drama in the National Curriculum includes improvised, unrehearsed role-play, as well as performance, such as the school play. This section deals mainly with the benefits of unrehearsed situations through which all pupils, including the less able, can develop language and communication skills.

Exploring social contexts

Children with language difficulties benefit from extending the contexts in which they use language. At the play stage, the role-play area changes into a dentist's or doctor's surgery, hospital, airport, shop, post office, bank, travel agent or any other scene. Children can dress up and let imaginative role-play take them into any world they wish.

Improvised drama

Setting up an improvised drama situation is a bit like plotting a novel. At least five elements need to be considered: place, time, character, relationship and conflict.

Conflict distinguishes improvisation from everyday role-play situations, and has a greater directive power to develop communicative competency through problem-solving. Conflict provides the problem to be resolved. Consider how the following areas of conflict could enhance communication skills:

- mending a broken friendship;
- reaching consensus from opposing points of view, e.g. on school uniform, capital punishment, what to do about vandalism;
- dealing with a racism issue; or
- exploring disability issues.

Improvisation could also help pupils to play a key part in school issues, e.g. homework – what kind, how much and why? In character, pupils who are shy, lack confidence, have speech problems or have low self-esteem can express themselves through the character whose skin they are wearing at the time. Drama can also develop what takes place in the literacy hour, the numeracy hour, or across the curriculum. Children could:

- act out the stories from 'big books';
- act out plays written during the literacy hour; or
- act out situations from cross-curricular work, e.g. to develop feelings of empathy for historical characters.

Drama provides scope for language work in large or small groups or as pairs. To engage all pupils as far as possible:

- organise the five areas first (place, time, character, relationship and conflict);
- ensure pupils know the goals of the activity;
- keep pupils on track, and avoid undirected chatter which fails to address the issues;
- trust pupils to get on by themselves and avoid interrupting; and
- provide the least able pupils with objects, pictures and so on to remind them, and help them to 'get into' their character.

Boys and drama

Strategies to address the under-achievement of boys are a priority on many LEA educational development plans. The Qualifications and Curriculum Authority (QCA 1998a), in a booklet entitled *Can Do Better: Raising Boys' Achievement in English* states that, 'Performance, improvisation and other drama activities are often favoured by boys . . . In Key Stage 2 drama is often a neglected aspect of the English curriculum. Teachers feel they lack confidence in teaching improvisation, and writing stories is much more common than writing and performing plays.' Reading and writing plays as part of the NLS non-fiction objectives could provide class or group drama material from literacy hour work.

'Boys can do better' alerted teachers to boys' styles of talk and their strengths. It is easy to favour girls or to undervalue what boys offer as communication. For example, boys may tend to make brief, more direct comments without elaboration. The above report suggested that any narrowing of the range required in the English National Curriculum programmes of study will affect more boys than girls. For example, 'If boys prefer to be active and doing, their ability to listen and respond may be underdeveloped.' Drama offers boys the opportunity to communicate in their own way and may support other areas of their learning. They enjoy the 'cut and thrust' of oral work.

Drama has the potential to move all pupils' language and communication forward and encourage positive relationships between children.

Poetry, literature and language

Talk about literature is talk about written language. A similar comment may be made about poetry, which could be inaccessible to some children unless it is talked about in depth, but could also be of great benefit to all children.

Literature

If literature is literacy at its most high-flying, what are the benefits, particularly for children with language difficulties? The Bullock Report (DfE 1975), *A Language for Life*, the most comprehensive manual about language and literacy ever written, suggests that, 'Literature brings the child into an encounter with language in its most complex and various forms. Through these complexities are presented the thoughts, experiences and feelings of people who exist outside and beyond the reader's daily awareness.'

Talking about literature helps to make the above comments more of a truism for children with language and communication problems. Focused talk about literature can:

- develop pupils' understanding about stories, their function and attributes, i.e. 'What is a story? What is a plot? Why has the story got a beginning, a middle and an end? What would happen if we took out the middle bit where the main character falls in the puddle?' and so on.
- help children to deal with emotions. Most literature has a theme, e.g. death, war, neglect and so on. Talking about literature is almost like dramatising the characters' emotions, and has the potential to help many children through emotional trauma.
- link in with subject work, e.g. a book set during the Second World War can help pupils to develop empathy with people's experiences during the war, and help them to appreciate history as a human story.
- help children with communication difficulties to explore and to understand themselves;
- help to develop appreciation of 'good' literature (i.e. talking about why a book is good, or not). Not all pupils reach such evaluative comprehension, yet can benefit from discussion provided they can engage with the interactive talk.

Beard (1987), as a sixth-former preparing for the teaching profession, relates how reading and talking about *Lord of the Flies* by William Golding made a tremendous impression on his beliefs about the primitive instincts which reside in civilised society. On a simpler note, both adults and children relate to the theme of *Not Now, Bernard* from Arrow (Red Fox). Literature can be for everyone.

Poetry and language

Not surprisingly, many less able children dislike poetry. The poem they are trying to enjoy and to analyse as part of the literacy hour may be beyond their understanding, or conflict with their language targets, e.g. pupils learning to speak in sentences. Listening to or reading out a poem can cause anxiety unless poetry is talked about. Talk could involve:

- why poetry is not written in sentences, to reassure pupils learning to 'speak in simple sentences' that poetry is different;
- thorough discussion of the images presented, with pictures or objects to aid understanding for some pupils: a poem about snow may need a picture of a snowy day;

- talking about the metaphors presented, as many pupils with poor language struggle to comprehend beyond the literal level;
- helping less able pupils to engage as far as possible by focusing on something they can respond to, e.g. clapping the syllables and sensing the rhythm of the language. Children may gain more from poetry by appreciating its rhymes and rhythms, even if they cannot access the depth of comprehension.

Literature and poetry in some form are valuable to all children. Talk is the medium through which those with language difficulties will benefit both linguistically and emotionally.

Communication through practical subjects

Practical areas of the curriculum have the potential to emphasise the 'doing' aspects of communication, and encourage children of all abilities to respond to specific elements of listening comprehension, such as details, or cause and effect.

Physical education (PE)

Apart from health and safety considerations in PE, children with language and communication difficulties need to understand instructions and other communication in order to benefit from it. Figure 6.4 lists some of the verb structures and prepositions which could cause difficulty for some children on a language programme.

How are children organised in PE? Are they in teams, as pairs, or as individuals? Pupils may need to be reminded, and supported by a picture, such as a card on the wall showing two stick people to represent a pair, or colours to represent a team. Activities in PE may involve a sequence, with potential difficulties for children who are learning to communicate with others by actions.

Instructions – Go! Walk slowly . . . quickly. Are you ready?
Jump three times on the spot. Now . . . hop on one leg. Crawl . . .
Touch . . . Stand still! Climb . . .
Prepositions – under, over, below, behind, between, in front of, in the middle of, on top of, up, down, etc.

Figure 6.4 Verbs and prepositions in PE

Suggestions for instructions:

- keep instructions simple – some pupils may only be able to cope with one step at a time;
- support instructions by a picture or word card, especially if the activity is to last for a few minutes;
- gain full attention before giving out an instruction;
- repeat the main words of the instruction if necessary; and
- reinforce and praise the correct responses.

Design and technology

Health and safety are a priority where children are required to use tools and materials which could harm themselves or others if handled incorrectly. Language and communication in design and technology invite the following questions:

- what are the rules for working with potentially dangerous tools or materials, e.g. cutting tools?
- have pupils been shown precisely how to handle them?
- how is the competence of children with language and communication difficulties in this area checked out? For example, how does a teacher know that the pupil understands the dangers, or knows how to hold a tool?
- do health and safety issues suggest the need for an LSA to support certain practical lessons?

Practical subjects make it necessary to view language and communication difficulties from a health and safety perspective as well as a learning perspective, and to use talk effectively to ensure safety alongside learning.

Information and Communication Technology (ICT)

The development of ICT also enables other learning. ICT facilitates the value and the purpose of talk, especially for pupils with severe communication difficulties. *The National Curriculum for Pupils with Severe Learning Difficulties* (NCC 1989c) reminds teachers how ICT aids communication. The range of ICT equipment currently available can:

- provide sensory stimulation, allowing pupils to generate visual and aural patterns using a single switch;
- develop the understanding of cause and effect through switch-operated toys;
- allow decision-making through 'yes' or 'no' switches;
- enable cooperation through programmes with two switches;
- facilitate participation in group activities by enabling pupils to produce 'writing' through pictures or symbols;
- minimise communication difficulties through programmes which scan symbol vocabularies in response to switch use; and
- stimulate creativity through the use of computer-generated artwork or music.

The list above indicates ICT equipment which is switch-operated for pupils unable to operate an ordinary computer independently. ICT has the potential to develop communication for all children; those with less severe language difficulties will also benefit from pair work on the computer. Chapter 9 offers further ideas for ICT resources.

From information to knowledge

Subject learning is about new knowledge. Information acquired through cross-curricular experiences only becomes knowledge when learners manipulate the information and make it their own. The Bullock Report (DfE 1975) suggested that children find out and gather information from a range of sources, which include observation and first hand experience; listening to explanations and discussion; listening to a spoken monologue (e.g. a lecture) and reading.

The above areas represent the receptive channels of communication, i.e. receiving information through language. Until information has been understood and assigned to the mind's unique filing system, ready to produce when required, it is not yet usable knowledge. But how does information become knowledge? Consider what we are actually doing when we:

- clarify new information with the person who presented it to ensure our understanding and respond in the right way;
- ask questions on training courses which either test our understanding of information or suggest a link between the new information and what we already know;

- look up an unfamiliar word in a dictionary; or
- ask questions to extend the information.

The above actions illustrate how we all turn information into knowledge. Children with language and communication difficulties need more support than the majority of learners to turn information into knowledge on their own terms. This applies to the massive amount of information communicated through diagrammatic formats which pupils need to understand if they are to respond to it.

Diagrammatic information

Consider the diagrammatic formats presented in Figure 6.5. Similar information forms part of every subject, causing confusion for many children, as it requires inferential comprehension which many less able children need help to develop. Talk offers a route through the maze.

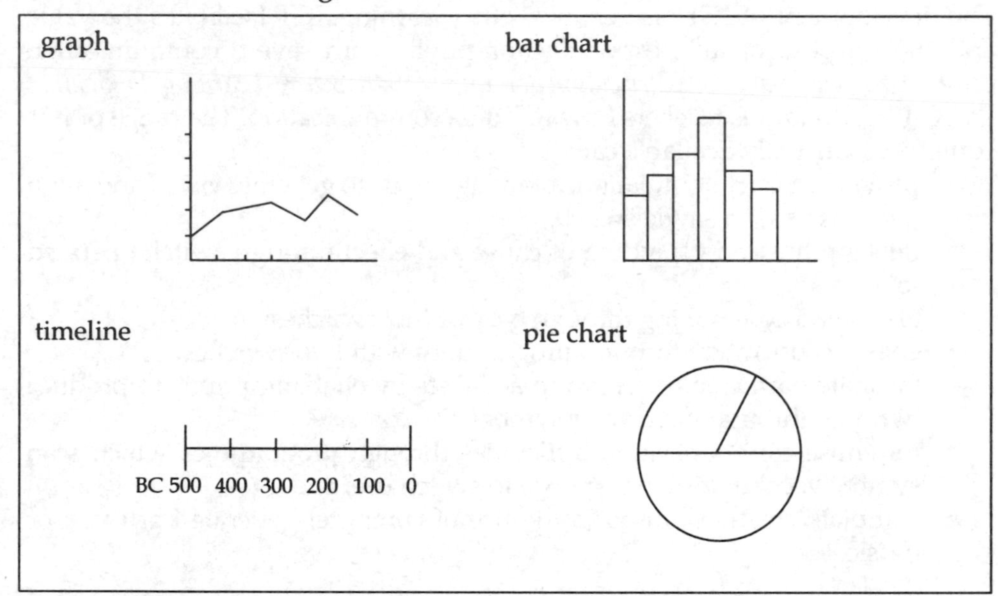

Figure 6.5 Diagrammatic formats

Consider a Venn diagram. Why are the two circles inter-connected? Talk can help pupils to understand the difference between data in the interconnecting section, and out of it. What about a bar chart? Children with difficulties in processing information will not automatically connect the two axes, nor will they infer meaning from the height of the bars. What are the numbers for? Similarly, the significance of the points on graphs and the implications for interpreting information may need to be thoroughly discussed.

Diagrams such as time lines rely on an understanding of sequence. Different spacing between significant dates often represents units of time in years, and may need to be talked about. Number lines are not easily interpreted by children with underdeveloped levels of understanding.

Suggested activities

Talking about diagrammatic formats can help children to develop their use of language as well as their understanding of the subject information presented. Apart from whole-class discussion, children could work in pairs or groups to:

- present their own information through a range of diagrams;
- explain their information to their partner, or to the group, saying why they chose that form of diagram;
- ask each other questions about different diagrams; or

- work from a list of teacher-directed questions to generate a group response to the diagrammatic information as illustrated in Figure 6.6.

Science – Bar chart to show how model cars travel on rough surfaces

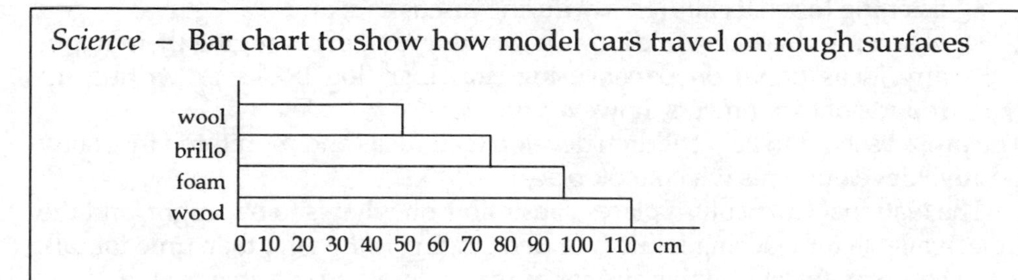

Questions:

1a. On which surface did the car travel furthest?
b. What does this tell us about this surface?
2a. On which surface did the car travel the least distance?
b. What does this tell you about this surface?
3. As a group note six different kinds of facts from the bar chart. (number scales? difference between wool and others? number of materials used?)
4. As a group, write down some more surfaces you could have used for the experiment. Talk about what results you would expect for each one. Why would you predict that result?

Figure 6.6 Responding to diagrammatic formats

Each group could present their response to a different diagram for the benefit of the class. One group may talk about their bar chart, followed by the next group explaining their pie chart. If work on reading or writing using diagrams has featured in the literacy or the numeracy hour, the plenary sections could use group activities to summarise the different functions of diagrammatic formats.

The difficulties of science

Science causes grave difficulties for many pupils at every key stage, and not only for those with language difficulties. The author of this book, a reasonably intelligent person, has encountered significant problems with science from the start, causing much of the subject to remain a mystery.

Why is science such a problem for many learners? An article in *Support for Learning* (Bell 1998) described the challenges faced by teachers of children with learning difficulties in primary schools, and efforts made to address them. The report contained many helpful observations and comments, among them a description of the SPACE approach to teaching and learning science. The SPACE project was a classroom-based research project, funded by the Nuffield Foundation, which ran from 1987 to 1991. The project was based on the view that children have to develop their ideas from their experiences, and that their existing ideas influence subsequent learning. We are reminded here of the Plowden principle (DfE 1967) of child-centred learning.

The project methodology included:

- exploration and development of scientific understanding as a key part of classroom activity;
- teachers responding to children's ideas more effectively, using strategies and approaches matched closely to pupils' needs; and
- research to improve the understanding of how conceptual development can be encouraged in the classroom.

Finding out what ideas children hold is a first, essential key to unlocking the door to science. The project included:

- listening to what children say during discussion; and
- observing children while they are working, and encouraging them to put any ideas down on paper, using drawings, log books or writing up reports of experiments, however simply.

The project set out to help children develop their ideas and monitored the many positive developments which took place.

The National Curriculum places constraints on what is to be taught, and the time available for teaching it but, if understanding is the aim, then time for talk is the best way to achieve this aim for as many pupils as possible.

Cross-curricular activities

The *NCC: Framework for the Primary Curriculum* (NCC 1989a) suggested that the aims of the National Curriculum are more likely to be achieved, 'where numeracy, literacy and oracy are given highest priority . . . and are soundly taught,' and where 'pupils are led to ask questions and seek answers individually and in cooperation with others, and their thinking is guided and informed . . . by teachers and other adults.' These comments also reflect education on the brink of a new millennium.

The final part of this chapter suggests how natural links between subject work can be exploited for the benefit of subject learning as well as for speaking and listening skills. To stimulate their integrated use of cross-curricular language, children could:

- talk about the famous landmarks of Germany, Italy or France (e.g. the Eiffel Tower), using pictures as stimuli (in modern foreign languages (MFL));
- compose a poem about an aspect of maths;
- devise games for aspects of number work and record them;
- dramatise historical events;
- role-play aspects of cultures studied in geography;
- talk about famous composers in music;
- discuss famous artists, using their work as stimuli;
- make models of buildings or structures from historical periods, e.g. Tudor houses, using both historical and technological language in the same context;
- use literature to elicit information about historical periods or events or different cultures;
- use PE and dance to talk about how living things move; and
- dramatise scientific achievement, and the struggles of scientists, e.g. Marie Curie, Louis Pasteur.

Module 6 of the NLS Training Pack (DfEE 1998c) focuses on reading and writing for information. For example, 'during the literacy hour, pupils might be searching and retrieving from information texts used in science, writing instructions linked to a technology topic, studying myths, autobiographies or stories linked to a study unit in history.'

The NLS emphasises the fundamental links of literacy across the curriculum, but stresses that, 'other subjects should . . . not displace (literacy) from its primary focus in the literacy hour (p13, *NLS: Framework for Teaching*; DfEE 1998b).

By using natural opportunities for subject work during the literacy hour, time is used to advantage. As an example from NLS Module 6 suggests, 'children might make notes on Roman towns during the literacy hour . . . concentrating (and talking about) the skills of effective notetaking. In a subsequent history session the notes could be used to make an accurate map or model of a typical Roman town.'

The Implementation of the National Numeracy Strategy (DfEE 1998e) stresses that:

> other subjects offer a rich source of opportunities for children to consolidate and practise what they have learned in maths lessons . . . children can read books that include mathematical data . . . in geography, children use co-ordinates, compass directions and bearings . . . In art, children can look at the properties of shapes and patterns . . . in PE children measure distance, time and speed.

All of the above are accomplished through the richness of talk. Speaking and listening, like reading and writing, are content free. Without subject information, what would there be to talk about?

Chapter 7

Talk in the Numeracy Hour

Mathematics Non-Statutory Guidance (NCC 1989b) described maths as 'a way of viewing and making sense of the world . . . used to analyse and communicate information and ideas, and to tackle a range of practical tasks and real-life problems. Maths has the capacity not just to describe and explain, but also to predict.'

Ten years on, those comments on the introduction of the National Curriculum are reflected in the objectives of the National Numeracy Strategy (NNS) which primary schools are expected to adopt from the autumn term of 1999. *The Implementation of the National Numeracy Strategy* (DfEE 1998e) describes numerate primary-aged pupils as, 'confident and competent enough to tackle problems without going immediately to teachers and friends for help.' Children should:

- have a sense of the size of a number and where it fits into the number system;
- know by heart number facts such as number bonds, multiplication tables, division facts, doubles and halves;
- use what they know by heart to figure out answers mentally;
- calculate accurately and efficiently, both mentally and on paper, drawing on a range of calculation strategies;
- recognise when it is appropriate to use a calculator . . . and be able to use one effectively;
- make sense of number problems, including non-routine problems, and recognise operations needed to solve them;
- explain their methods and reasoning using correct mathematical terms;
- judge whether their answers are reasonable, and have strategies for checking them where necessary;
- suggest suitable units for measuring and make sensible estimates of measurements; and
- explain and make predictions from the numbers in graphs, diagrams, charts and tables.

Where do speaking and listening skills feature in the NNS? The preliminary report, *Numeracy Matters* (DfEE 1998d) stressed the importance of oral work as a key factor in the successful teaching of mathematics and numeracy. The NNS recommends a model of whole-class teaching, with carefully organised group work. If pupils are to make sense of the mathematical world, they should receive teaching that:

- instructs and demonstrates, explains and illustrates mathematics;
- maximises teacher and pupil interaction, so that pupils can talk and be listened to, and receive feedback that helps them to develop their mathematical knowledge, skills and understanding; and
- allows pupils to . . . explain their thinking and methods, and suggest alternative ways of tackling problems.

Numeracy Matters (DfEE 1998d) stresses talk as central to the teaching and learning process, echoing the language and communication skills of 'effective questioning techniques' and 'clear instruction', among other speaking and listening strategies.

Numeracy in Action (BBC TV 1998) illustrated a number of techniques for developing mathematical understanding. Through class activities, children are encouraged to:

- challenge and question;
- explore (e.g. place value – which digit is important?);
- test out information to see if it fits the objective ('Shall we check that these three coins make 50p?'); and
- demonstrate their knowledge ('Show me a multiple of 10 that is less than 30').

The class-based strategy aims to ask one question and get five back, stimulating children's questioning techniques. During the group session, children are using what they have learned to explore further, practice or test out what they have learned during the class session. In the plenary, children may share ideas that have worked well, and talk about problems their group has experienced.

Effective numeracy begins well before children arrive in school. *Desirable Outcomes for Mathematics* (SCAA 1996), extracts of which are listed in Figure 7.1, provide the foundations of numeracy which all children need in order to access the NNS from the reception year of schooling. Note the emphasis on speaking and listening as the medium through which the desirable outcomes are to be achieved.

Children:

- use mathematical language . . . to describe shape, position, size and quantity;
- recognise and recreate patterns;
- compare, sort, match, order, sequence and count, using everyday objects;
- begin to . . . solve practical problems;
- show awareness of number operations; and
- begin to use the language involved.

Figure 7.1 Extracts from *Desirable Outcomes for Mathematics* (SCAA 1996)

Developing mathematical language

Having spoken to children with learning difficulties about their perceptions of maths, the majority appear to think maths exists mainly in school books or on worksheets. A major reason why some children have not progressed is because they have not linked 'school maths' to its practical applications in the home and around their environment.

The desirable outcomes for mathematical learning during the early years provide the essential starting points and mathematical vocabulary essential for success through the NNS. Children with language and communication difficulties, and other forms of learning difficulty, need ample opportunities to ask questions and reach understanding. All mathematics needs to be first developed through the context in which it is used.

Where is maths?

Maths and mathematical language is everywhere. In the home we get up (time), have breakfast (match spoons, cups, know which size of bowl fits the cereal), make meals (weighing), do the washing, go shopping and so on. People go to the doctor's, go shopping, go on holiday or out to leisure parks, all of which uses maths. Consider the language of everyday activities:

1. Number and early experiences – how many stairs are there? Let's count them (on the way to bed). How many eggs have we got? One is broken . . . let's throw it away. How many are left?
2. Time – breakfast will be ready in half an hour. What time is it? How long will the cake take to cook? How long will the washing take? Fast or slow?

3. Length – do we need a long piece or a short one? Which is the longest/shortest? How wide/long is a roll of wallpaper? How many rolls will we need?
4. Shapes – what shape is the cake tin? Circular or square? Draw a plan of your doll's house/garage etc. What shapes can you see?
5. Capacity – is the bowl full, empty, or half-full? Which jug holds most or least? Does the jar hold more than the cup? What if the jar was smaller?
6. Weight – this packet is heavy, but this is heavier. Does heavier or lighter always equate with more or less?
7. Money – how much does it cost? Have we enough? How much more do we need?
8. Other areas, e.g. fractions – cut the cake into quarters, eighths etc.

Maths is everywhere! El-Naggar (1994) describes a maths trail as the parallel to a nature trail. Maths trails could be a way of enhancing interest and helping to lift maths out of the confines of the classroom. Maths trails are school-based explorations of maths around the environment. The idea is that pupils experience maths from questions and instructions, related to what they see along the trail – notice boards, railings, windows, steps, litter bins, car parks, e.g. 'Do you think the car park is full? Half-full? A quarter full?' Imagine the amount of mathematical talk on a maths trail.

Addressing language difficulties in maths

Children with speaking and listening difficulties need to work more intensively on the range of language areas and be taught to cue in to the different facets of understanding. Talk in maths will revolve around questions and answers, instructions and responses, as well as statements which contain information to support problem-solving activities. Ensure pupils can distinguish the purposes of mathematical talk. Teach the differences between:

- *Questions* – what time is it? How many . . . ? Which contains most? Which pencil is the longest?
- *Instructions* – draw a square. Draw a line from corner to corner. Put a cross in one half . . . and so on; and
- *Statements of information* – 'A square has four corners and four sides.' Show pupils how statements of information (written and verbal) are usually followed by questions or instructions.

Through modelling, show examples of different responses to the kinds of sentences above, for example, through oral question and answer work, or verbal instructions, delivered at appropriate levels of language difficulty.
Direct pupils' attention to:

1. Detail – all of maths relies on understanding the details of a question, instruction or statement. Apart from estimation, the correct outcome of most mathematical activities relies on pupils having listened to (or read) and understood the precise details from the language, and interpreted its message in terms of what they have to do.
2. Sequence – counting starts from an understanding of sequence. Sequence and order form a large part of life, and are a constant source of difficulty. Pupils who have not realised the importance of sequence – in numbers,time and so on, cannot develop their mathematical understanding.
3. Comparison – shorter/longer, taller/shorter, more than/less than. The comprehension skills of comparison feature in many areas of maths.
4. Cause and effect – if we add a number there will be more. If we take it away there will be less. What is the effect of adding, subtracting, multiply ing or dividing on a given number? When we move the decimal point what is the effect? What mathematical operation has caused that number to halve?

The examples illustrate that maths relies on thinking skills in concert with those of language. Consider the matches puzzle presented in Chapter 1. Pupils with poor understanding of language will struggle to build upon each stage of mathematical thinking, without specific instruction on areas of comprehension such as those highlighted above. Children with SLD need to be taught to cue in to details, sequence and so on, to secure those elements of language, e.g. getting changed before and after PE – 'what shall we put on first/next/after that/before this?'

Problem-solving

For many children, the instruction to 'close your maths books,' means that mathematical thinking has ceased, as maths exists only in the maths lesson. Many negative pupil attitudes to maths and numeracy are about to be changed by the introduction of the numeracy hour, as children see maths in a new light, as problem-solving.

Why is it that a child can multiply five by eight, yet may struggle to work out the problem: if a box contains five toy cars, how many toy cars are contained in eight boxes? Many teachers will recall some very illogical answers to a recent National Curriculum assessment problem of how many buses were needed for a school trip – the answer 'two and a half' came up frequently!

Addressing the problem

1. Teach pupils how to solve maths problems. Start with simple problems with one mathematical step – Pat has five sweets. She drops one. How many has she left? Build up according to children's number levels and language skills.
2. Write a problem to be solved on an OHP or a whiteboard to help pupils remember what the class is talking about.
3. Show the least able pupils how to apply subtraction to the problem by modelling – blu-tack five paper sweets onto the board, drop one, and ask pupils to count how many are left.
4. Cue pupils' attention to what is about to be said – 'Now listen to this instruction/question. What is . . . ?'
5. Stress the details during oral work – 'Think carefully. If John is EIGHT, and his sister Katie, is THREE YEARS YOUNGER . . . HOW OLD is Katie?'
6. Use the names of less able or less motivated children as part of the model ling, and involve them as visual aids – 'Pat, Mark and John are a set of boys with brown hair' (children standing at the front of the class).

Case studies

Lisa's problem

Lisa hated fractions because she always got them wrong. The source of the problem emerged one day when she was talking to her teacher (me) about the wrong answers. Until we had talked about it, and uncovered the difficulty, Lisa saw $^1/_4$ as smaller than $^1/_5$ because she was thinking of them as numbers. Talking about why $^1/_5$ is called a fifth, i.e. because it is a whole number (one) shared into five parts enabled her to move forwards.

Many children struggle with fractions because they fail to understand their fundamentals. Only talk can uncover muddled perceptions. Part of the talk which enabled Lisa's leap towards understanding is transcribed in Figure 7.2.

Lisa:	A quarter's smaller . . . four . . . it's less than five.
Mrs E:	Let's have a look at this . . . Share 20p between four people on this table.
Group discussion followed about sharing into four.	
Mrs E:	Now, why have you each got a quarter of 20p?
Lisa:	Because . . . we've shared into four.
Mrs E:	Right . . . share 20p between five (using 10 x 2p coins) How much have you each got now?
Lisa:	4p . . . it's less than before.
Group discussion followed . . . of five people and fifths.	
Mrs E:	Why is a fifth less than a quarter?
Lisa:	I think it's because we've got five people now, so we've all got less . . . more shares. If we shared into ten, we'd have 2p . . . would we have a tenth?

Figure 7.2 Lisa – moving forward with fractions

Barry's problem

Barry had supplied the wrong answer to a mathematical test question, along the lines of 'a table has four legs; how many legs have five tables?' The task was not to find the answer, but to state the correct operation. Barry's response was 'addition'. The required response was 'multiplication'. When asked, Barry gave the correct answer to the problem (20), and showed me his working out, as addition, by slowly counting each table leg from his drawing. Further talk enabled Barry to see the relationship between addition and multiplication, and that multiplication enables us to work with larger numbers.

Dawn's problem

Dawn (Year 9) was trying to divide 65.46 by 10, and was desperately trying to remember the method demonstrated by the teacher. She mumbled something about, 'a point . . . need to move the point' and that, 'ten has a nought in it,' but could not connect these thoughts. In the end, she moved the point the wrong way, having multiplied instead of divided.

Dawn's struggle, and the talk which accompanied it, showed that she had not fully grasped place value, and how decimals relate to whole numbers. The teacher had attempted to help by giving her a method but, as Dawn has been assessed as having specific learning difficulties (SpLD), confuses left and right and has a poor memory, the method was not working.

Talking about maths and numeracy helps to tease out the sources of children's difficulties and to approach the problem from the learners' perceptions. Maths is thinking. Without understanding, there can be no thought.

We all think differently. How would you mentally work out 5 multiplied by 4.6? I multiplied by 10 first, got 46, then halved it. Others may multiply 5 by 4, then 5 by 0.6, then add both answers together. Understanding of numeracy is helped by having different methods to choose from. The more opportunities children have to talk through different ways of working out problems, at the right level, the more flexible their thinking will become. All maths involves thinking and problem-solving. The aim of the NNS is to enable children to talk about and understand maths as part of life.

Chapter 8

Organising Focused Language Activities

Language is both caught and taught. Immersing children in a rich and creative language and communication environment is not enough for all of them; learners with underdeveloped language need focused activities with adults and peers as part of a planned programme. Previous chapters have explored language and communication through other areas of learning, e.g. through the literacy and numeracy hours, and across the curriculum. This chapter considers how speaking and listening in their own right are developed through focused activities matched to group or individual learning targets.

Talking about talk

If speaking and listening skills are to improve, all children need to know that talk is important. Many children appear to think that if neither reading nor writing has featured in a lesson, they have not 'worked'. All children need to perceive talk as an important area of their learning. Two examples from the National Oracy Project (NCC 1991, 1993) below focus on children's attitudes to talk as part of school-based learning, and links with home.

Example 1

Talk in the Reception class aimed to, 'raise the status of talk' by making it the feature of a class topic. Two teachers with similar mixes of pupils combined their efforts for a joint project and brainstormed some areas of speaking and listening. Figure 8.1 reproduces the web of talk areas which initiated the 'talk' topic.

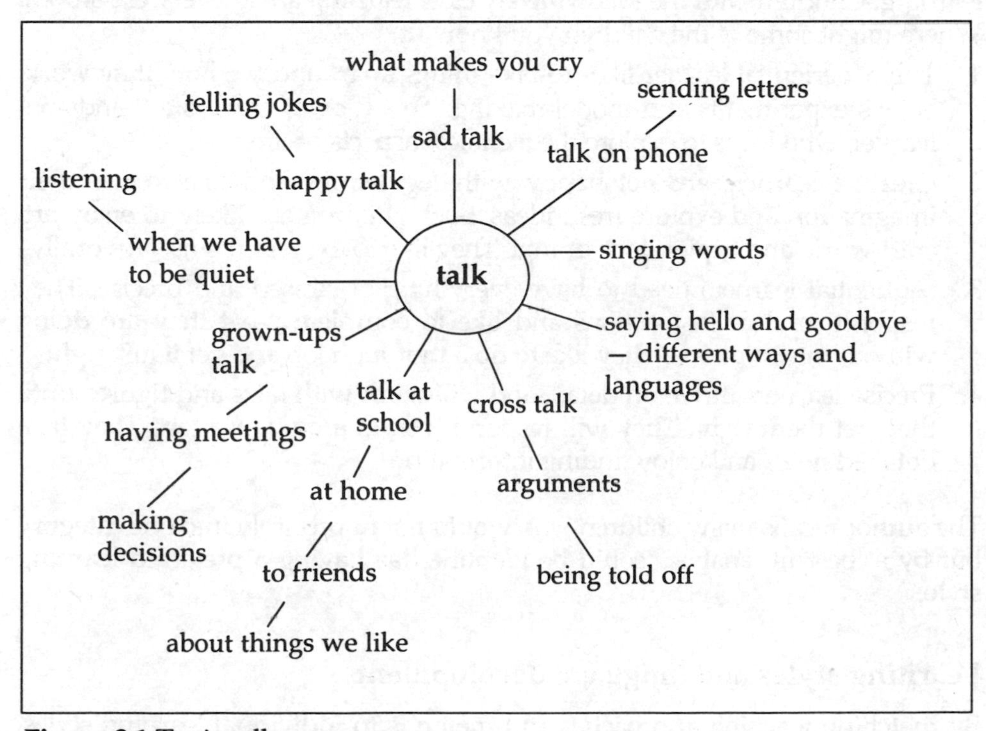

Figure 8.1 Topic talk

The teachers introduced the ideas to their respective classes to invite their responses. The teachers commented, 'We were surprised at the sophistication of their knowledge . . . being able to isolate areas of talk which interested them, including 'how grown-ups talk' and 'making decisions and having meetings'. With a wealth of ideas, the children were then allowed to lead the investigation into various areas of talk. The areas of talk activity were as diverse as:

- happy and sad talk, using photographs and tapes;
- exploring other mother tongues in the classroom; and
- talking about maths – what makes maths talk different?

The article goes on to describe the value of the topic and the enhanced status of talk in both classrooms.

Example 2

Teddy Topics used Year 1 children's own teddy bears as an imaginative way of giving reasons for talk. The children were asked to bring their teddies into school and to talk about them. The teacher commented, 'Some of the children spoke about physical aspects . . . "He is yellow, he has orange eyes." Others seemed to concentrate more on what their teddies could do. "My Teddy understands words and English. He is called Big Ted. He is a daddy."' This teacher goes on to explain how the teddies 'sat down to do work', and 'fell in the mud' etc. The point of this example is how favourite playthings can effectively link talk in school with the home. Accompanied by the story of *Goldilocks and the Three Bears*, the teddy topic stimulated work on mathematical language.

Both examples illustrate the way in which talk enhances learning and is itself enhanced by it.

Looking at learning styles

Activities aimed at developing speaking and listening start from a child's needs. Particularly through the early years, and through Key Stage 1, adults need to observe children in a range of situations – practical activities, playing, talking in a group, and so on, gauging and responding to children's preferred styles of learning. Children with the following styles of learning are in every classroom. Where might some of the children you know fit?

1. The experiential learner likes to take things apart and see how they work, enjoys experiments and model-making. This type of child is a 'hands-on' learner, who loves to explore the technical aspects of life.
2. Creative learners are not happy with regulations and like to use their imagination and explore fresh ideas. Such children are likely to enjoy art, craft-work, and exploratory drama. They like to express themselves orally.
3. Sequential learners need to have everything organised and precise. They respond to clear instructions and like to complete what they are doing without interruptions. They like to do a thorough job and get it just right.
4. Precise learners thrive on detail, and will work with facts and figures until they get them right. They will respond well to a quiz or a test. They take detailed notes and enjoy finding information.

The author recalls many children who would not fit precisely into one category but by a 'best fit' analysis could be identified as having a preferred learning style.

Learning styles and language development

By matching teaching approaches and methods to individual learning styles, teaching is more likely to result in learning. If a child loves to build and make models then, during the focused activities, use that approach to stimulate interest and guide the language teaching accordingly. If another child prefers order and routine, then focused work can allow this type of learner to work from clear instructions and finish work properly to his own satisfaction. Focused teaching could allow the creative child to develop language through art, stories and imaginative approaches, while still emphasising skills to be learned.

Activities with an adult, or with peers, which are focused on a child's IEP, offer opportunities when a child's preferred learning style could guide the teaching.

Focused language work

There is no substitute for language development in a context of meaningful experience, where a child is stimulated to communicate and learn alongside his peer group. Tuning children in to the significance of talk, as exemplified by the examples from the National Oracy Project, helps to prepare children for the structured language work which focuses more precisely on individual or group needs.

Identifying the purpose

Structured language activities need a focus to prevent the talk degenerating into a general ramble. If focused talk is to be assessed we need to know what it is intended to achieve. It is worth reflecting on the variety of ways in which speaking and listening activities can be organised, with regard to their overall function. Is the child developing his ability to describe, entertain, explain, solve, evaluate, criticise, report, plan, hypothesise and so on.

According to the purpose of a language-focused activity, children are organised in different ways, to talk in pairs, in small groups, to a small audience, to the whole class, to another class, and to a visitor. Audience combinations can move between known and unknown peers and adults to offer a variety of talk experiences.

Social situations and role-play

Role-play can help children to appreciate the significance of social situations, and appropriate language to be used in each situation. Children with language delay may need to develop their flexibility with language through role-play more intensively and for longer than their more accomplished peers. Consider each of the following social situations as the focus of language development and appropriate etiquette:

- cooking and preparing meals;
- having breakfast;
- going to the hospital/doctor/dentist;
- having a meeting;
- going shopping/to the bank/taking the car to be serviced; or
- having an important visitor for tea.

If the focus of the activity is on having visitors, the notion of entertaining needs to be understood. The language used will vary according to the visitor, and may need to include terms of politeness — sit down, hello, how nice to see you, do come in etc. One of my groups decided to have the Queen to tea. Needless to say, the language used became quite 'posh', as one child described it. This could be one way of developing children's understanding of the difference between standard English and informal talk at local community level.

Role-play situations can be as controlled as the purpose of the activity suggests. If the needs of the children require particular categories of vocabulary or thought-processing to be brought into play, then role-play situations can be more structured; for example, having a visitor can be split up into:

- getting ready for the visitor – baking buns, setting the table, tidying up;
- greeting the guest – what do you say? and
- clearing away when the visitor has left.

The point of this section is to illustrate how a focus on particular language can be accomplished through role-play, either to practise vocabulary taught by an adult during a previous session, or to use carefully-chosen peer groups to develop each other's vocabulary.

If the role-play is to be controlled, it may be necessary to plan a few short dialogues to cue in less able children. Props help to set the scene. Following a slight accident outside our school, children chose to role-play the policeman talking to the two car drivers, and the policeman's hat was an essential prop to enhance his 'status'. Access to role-play for all children is important, but least able children may need pictures and objects, and possibly cue cards with their main words, depending on the level of support needed.

Focused activities with an adult

The following sections describe focused activities which have worked effectively with particular groups of children.

Focusing on thought processes

If the aim is to develop the thought processes which drive language, the following structure has been found useful, provided children have some basic vocabulary to start with. Activities to extend language could be based around the following:

- identification – it's a cat;
- description – black, small, large, has soft fur;
- action or function – what does it do/what is it for?
- comparison – smaller than an elephant/bigger than a . . . ;
- categorisation – an animal, wild or domestic? and
- manipulation – the 'what if' element, projecting the thought processes and extending the learner's imagination.

The aim is to extend language by leading the child's thought processing into a range of contexts, e.g. at the zoo, or in the post office, as illustrated in Figure 8.2. Ideally, language development accompanies direct experience, but some children have limited experience of their language environment. If the focused talk takes place in school, then objects, pictures and other items which help to portray the context are essential. Needless to say, some experiences, e.g. of wild animals, are less easy to recreate than others, but the video age has made it easier to compensate for language disadvantage and to offer children a glimpse into other worlds, in this case, through wildlife programmes.

Focusing on question words

Focused activities could be structured around the basic question words all children need – what, who, which, where, when, how and why. Activities could include:

- stimulating pictures – inviting questions and answers, children could take turns to ask questions, while the adult observes and assesses; and
- stories – questioning children about stories or inviting children to ask their own questions.

Thought process	At the zoo	In the post office
Identification What is it?	It's a lion.	It's a stamp/
Description What does it look/smell like?	Big and furry Yellow and brown	Sticky, square Has a picture on
Action/function What does it do? What is it for? How does it work?	It bites. It can run fast. It catches other animals to eat.	It's how we pay to send letters.
Comparison Is it like a . . . ? How is it different?	Bigger than our cat and our dog. Not as big as an elephant.	They have different prices on because . . .
Categorisation What does it belong with?	It's an animal. It's wild like the tiger.	Envelopes, notepads
Manipulation What if?	. . . it got out of its cage?	. . . the postman forgets to collect the letters?

Figure 8.2 Developing language through thought processing

Any question sends thought processing into different directions. Children need to know what kind of answer is inferred from the question. For example:

- *what* invites recall of an event, action, happening;
- *who* usually refers to a person;
- *when* refers to time of day, year, season or whatever is mentioned in the story or portrayed in the picture;
- *where* refers to the setting – cafe, home, beach, African plain, ocean; and
- *how* and *why* exploit the means and the purpose of an event or happening.

Many children with poor understanding are helped by focusing on the range of responses inferred from question words.

Further priorities for focused activities

Focused language activities may be driven by other priorities, for example:

- frequency of language use, e.g. words needed for a subject topic, words used in group games, words for PE safety;
- priority of children's immediate needs, e.g. to express the need to visit the toilet and other social necessities; and
- difficult structures, e.g. elements of grammar – plurals, negatives, different tenses.

Games for language work

Structured language work must never be boring. The following activities are useful for developing areas of language.

1. *Question games or activities*

(a) Write question words on cards, and prepare a range of response cards (pictures or written), as shown in Figure 8.3. Children have to match the question cards with response cards. The aim is to develop understanding of the kinds of responses required by each question; thus a 'who' question will be matched by a card showing people, a 'where' card could be matched by a picture of a beach (with no people on it). A picture of an occupied cafe could be matched by a 'who' or a 'where' card. The value of this activity arises from groups talking about the matches made, and why. Different groups could have cards to match ability levels, e.g. the least able groups could work with picture response cards.

(b) Children start a question for others to complete or ask questions for others to answer.

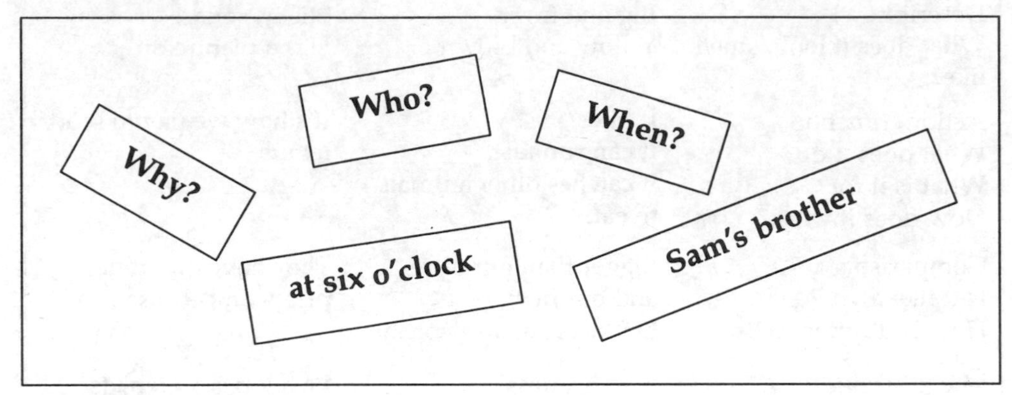

Figure 8.3 Question game

2. *Naming games and activities*

(a) Children sort mixed pictures or objects into those with the same name or attribute, e.g. chairs, dresses, balls. Played as a game, the first child to collate a given number of pictures could be the winner.

(b) Kim's game is a common way of developing naming and memory at the same time. Familiar objects are placed on the table, then taken away one, or a few, at a time depending on children's abilities. Children have to recall the name of the object removed. If they recall it, they could 'win' it.

(c) Feely bag – children feel into a bag with different objects and identify them by their shape and other attributes.

(d) I spy – this game is often used to develop phonic work, e.g. alliteration, but can also develop naming skills. For example, using objects around the room or on a table, or assorted pictures:

'I spy something beginning with . . .'
'I spy something round and soft . . .'
'I spy something we write with . . .'

(e) Bingo can help to develop naming skills. Each child has a bingo card with up to six pictures on it, e.g. of wild animals, items in the kitchen, or whatever language category is being focused on. The 'caller' has a set of single pictures to match the bingo card pictures. As the adult, or child 'caller' if playing as a group, holds up a picture, the first child to name it can cover it up on his bingo card. The first child to cover all pictures on his card wins.

3. *Description games and activities*

(a) 'I spy' also develops description language, focused on the target vocabulary to be learned – e.g. colour, size, shape, or a mixture: 'I spy something long, green and soft . . .'

(b) Sorting a range of items into colours, shapes, etc.

(c) Dressing up – children describe the different clothing.

(d) Through drama children can describe people as if they are witnesses to a burglary or an accident.

(e) Activities with actions – children take turns to describe a particular action, while others in the group mime it. Opening a parcel can be done – slowly, excitedly (e.g. a Christmas present), with fear etc. Walking around the room can be done slowly, quickly, sadly, excitedly. Different elements of grammar can be actioned through group activity.

4. *Categorisation games*

(a) Talk about and sort pictures into sets and sub-sets, e.g. clothes for winter, summer, holidays, playing outside and so on.

(b) Happy families – have cards for categories, e.g. animals, homes, furniture. Share them between the players. Place a pile of picture cards to match each category card, face-down on the table, in the centre. Children take turns to turn over one picture card at a time. If it belongs to their set, the child wins it. The first child to collect a given number of picture cards for his set wins the game.

5. *Sentence games*
(a) Start a sentence chain around the group. A child provides the first word, and children take turns to add a word. Sentences could be required to include certain elements of grammar, e.g. adjectives, adverbs, prepositions.
(b) True or false – a child makes a statement, accompanied by an action, e.g. the red pencil is on the left of the blue one (child having put it in that position). The next child, or group, talks about whether the statement is true or false. Taking turns around the group, children rearrange items, and make fresh statements using position, colour and so on to catch each other out.
(c) Children in groups take turns to give simple instructions to group members. From items on the table, and armed with paper and pencils, instructions could include:
    Draw a line about 6 cm long (using estimation as well);
    Pick up two red and three blue crayons; or
    Put on the red and green hat (from items on the table).
(d) Yes or no? Children take turns to ask questions at a suitable level of challenge for others, e.g. 'Can a bird swim?' 'Is the sun blue?' The response, if negative, could turn the question into a correct statement, e.g. 'No, the sun is yellow'.
(e) Silly sentences – a teacher or child says a silly sentence, e.g. 'John put on his shoes, then his socks and went downstairs'. Children have to make the sentence sensible.

The virtue of games is that they generate more games, and can be adapted for all kinds of uses. Children will happily play or prepare exciting language games during wet breaks, as well as focused language time. The activity of inventing the games also helps to develop language, as the problem-solving process explores a further dimension of 'what if . . . '.

Activities which develop language in a multi-sensory way retain interest; for example those which combine talk with different actions. Many games can also be organised to develop literacy or mathematical skills, e.g. an instruction to draw a line of a given length using estimation, or a language game which uses word cards. The point of the above examples is to stimulate thoughts on the range of language skills which can be developed by the creative use of games.

Planning language activities

Focused language activities are planned around children's IEP targets, but need a framework. Figure 8.4 illustrates a possible framework for planning, based on four main areas of language and communicative development.

All-purpose vocabulary

All-purpose vocabulary comprises the general language used in any context. Words of colour, size, shape or position add to the precision of language at sentence level. Without all-purpose vocabulary, language is stripped of its clarity and vividness, and sentences are bare – imagine your own use of language without prepositions or words of colour and size.

All-purpose vocabulary	Content vocabulary
colour, size, shape prepositions greetings, social	subject words topic words literacy, numeracy words
Language context	**Function words**
audience formality purpose of talk standard English	e.g. in, on, the, and question words – when, how elements of grammar

Figure 8.4 A framework for structured language activities

Content vocabulary

Content vocabulary includes words needed for the literacy and numeracy hours and the subject curriculum. Content words also include vocabulary from the home and around the environment. These are the meaning-carrying words, which should be lifted from texts when note-making. Content vocabulary usually forms pictures or actions in the mind, and carries its own meaning – book, coffee, Viking, paper, division, shape, square, house.

Function words

In contrast to content words, function words have little inherent meaning, but provide the necessary precision which turns content and all-purpose vocabulary into language – in, on, when, and, then, he. Many of these words are contained in the NLS high-frequency lists. In order to read and spell them, a child must be able to use them and know their function in sentence work.

Language context

The development of all-purpose, content and function vocabulary is limited without the context in which the language is used. Subject vocabulary needs to be presented in its context, using pictures or actual experiences, if new words are to make sense to children with language difficulties. In the numeracy hour, mathematical language gains precise meaning. Figure 8.5 illustrates the diversity of contexts for environmental language work, with much overlap and cross-referencing: for words to have meaning, they must be presented, practised and communicated in context.

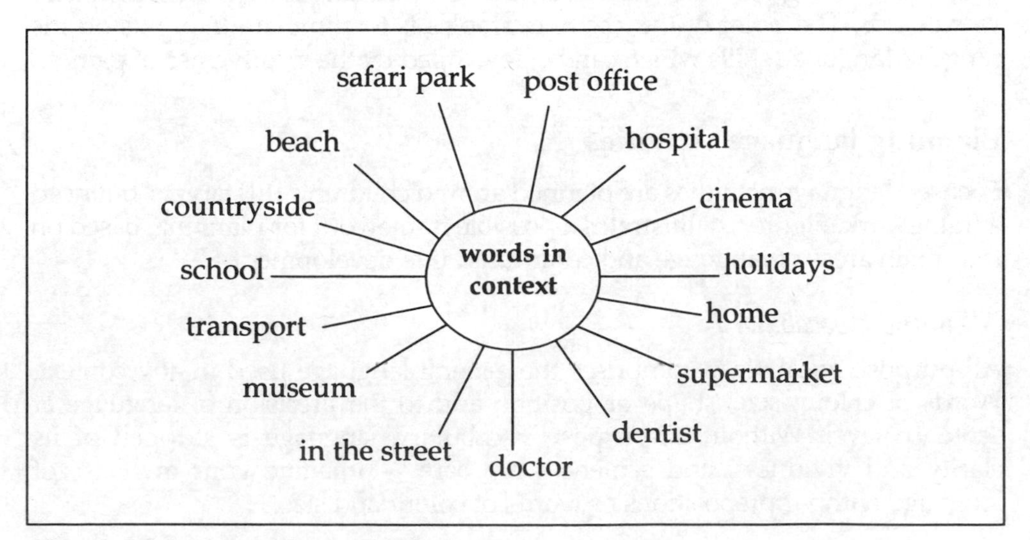

Figure 8.5 A range of contexts for language

Figure 8.4 offers a planning model to ensure that all four strands of growth feature as part of focused activities.

Activities for speaking and listening

A programme for developing language use may need to focus more on the skills of effective listening and speaking than on language itself.

Developing listening skills

Where children know the purpose for listening, and can engage with what is being said, they are less likely to switch off. Sharpen up pupils' listening skills by the following tasks:

1. Instructional activities, e.g. drawing from precise details, moving around the room, or 'Simon says' activities.
2. Stories - listening skills are enhanced when:
   - the story is at a suitable access and interest level;
   - it is read with expression and intonation;
   - pupils join in at intervals; and
   - questions are asked which bring out key points.
3. Clear and precise explanations of tasks take account of children's levels of understanding. Main meaning-carrying words should be stressed, and instructions should be:
   - limited to one activity at once, to avoid overloading the child's memory, e.g. not 'Get out your spelling book, turn to a fresh page, and fold it in half', at the same time; and
   - children's understanding of the listening should be checked, e.g. 'Now John, what have I said/what have you got to do?'

Auditory discrimination

Listening involves the ability to discriminate between what is heard. Children who are taught to distinguish between a range of sounds are more likely to transfer those skills to phonological awareness. Sounds could include common classroom noises, different musical instruments, animal noises, different voices, old and young, fast and slow sounds, rhythmic sounds, e.g. a train, vehicle sounds and sounds with a background of music.

Ordinary sounds such as writing on the blackboard, switching on lights or knocking on a door help to sharpen up auditory skills to support focused work on phonological awareness and other reading skills. Discrimination of similar words will also help; for example, which grows on birds — feathers or sweaters?

Developing speaking skills

Manolson (1992) suggests that children's language is actively developed by adding to what the child has said. Suggestions are aimed at parents, but the points made apply to any situation where the objective is to develop spoken language, particularly when working with children who have learning difficulties. Adding to language involves:

- using facial expressions and gestures;
- imitating what the child does, and adding a word or action connected to this;
- interpreting a child's feelings or wants;
- exaggerating sounds or key words;
- repeating the same words or phrases; and
- expanding on what the child is doing or saying.

In the context of the nursery, classroom, or during group activities much of what we do is instant and instinctive, as there is little time to plan responses to language. The principle of adding to what a child says by clarifying, repeating, expanding and so on could serve as a simple and practical guide to developing children's speaking skills.

Promoting thinking skills

Thinking skills are developed by the use of key phrases which promote specific thought processes. Examples of these key phrases for different thought processes are listed below.

1. Interpretation

describe in your own words translate compare/contrast what does it mean? how do you feel about? explain what are the relationships?

2. Application and making use of knowledge

demonstrate use it to solve . . . where does this lead to?

3. Analysis (breaking down the problem)

what are the causes/consequences? specify the criteria which is first/next/last? give me examples of list the problems

4. Synthesising (putting together and creating)

make create think of as many examples as you can how many different ways are possible? form a new . . . in what ways can you prove . . . ?

5. Evaluation

which are the best value? is this the best you can do? will it work? rate from good to poor

Thinking and language drive each other. While actively developing children's vocabulary levels, we need to develop the thinking skills which enable them to use language more effectively.

Strategies for children with learning difficulties

Teaching strategies for developing language for the least able children need to be carefully considered. A child with severe learning difficulties (SLD) needs to follow a basic programme guided by the stages of speech formation. Locke (1998) expands on the following areas of communication which must be slowly introduced:

- social referencing – establishing an awareness of people and things as the first evidence as intentional communication;
- early gestures – reach out, show, give and point;
- words and gestures – the ability to make one thing represent something, through signing or words; and
- words alone – once a child has single words, two-word utterances can soon follow.

The development of each stage for children with SLD may take months. Certain strategies facilitate the process, and apply to all language work:

- build communication through things of immediate interest, e.g. toys or food;
- making it difficult to open a box can encourage a child to make his wants known by word or gesture; and
- social routines, such as turn-taking, provide a context for requesting and commenting.

Pictures and objects with physical and verbal prompts encourage communication. Locke (1998) comments on the importance of continued attention to spontaneous sounds, joint attention with adults, non-verbal communication, symbolic play and adult responsivity as keys to the gradual production of words.

Communicative behaviour

So far, this chapter has looked at speaking and listening from the language perspective. For many children, focused activities may need to include the social behaviour which enables speaking and listening to achieve its outcome.

Circle time

Circle time is established as a means of developing communicative behaviour. The technique is usually thought of as a behaviour strategy, the aim being to raise self-esteem, but it has the potential to encourage all children to develop the kind of behaviour which facilitates good communication.

An example from the National Oracy Project (NCC 1991) describes how circle time proved to be a useful technique. The teacher explains:

> In a Reception/Year One class circle time takes place each morning . . . After a few minutes the circle is complete. The teacher . . . quietens the circle by stating that she has the magic microphone and that we always listen to whoever is holding it. The microphone is passed from person to person giving everyone a chance to contribute or pass. Some copy the teacher, some pass, some want to give more than one reason why, some say they are sad while smiling, some trustingly expose their feelings.

The teacher went on to comment how circle time has not only raised self-esteem, but has also helped to develop speaking and listening skills. A rule of circle time is that everyone has a right to be listened to, so only one person can speak at a time.

In another class of eight to ten-year-olds, circle time involves a more sophisticated use of talk. Children have developed their own version of circle time, with the teacher as one of the group. Various areas of talk ensue, e.g. 'What maths happened to you before you came to school?' The teacher commented on the many benefits:

- it is a structured way of giving each child the opportunity to speak and be listened to;
- a shy child can think of something to say without feeling threatened, yet more confident children can respond at a level appropriate to them;
- as it takes place within a structured format, children find it easier to listen as they know that their turn will come round; and
- it provides a means of allowing children to articulate their feelings, and ideas on any area of learning.

Group games and activities

Most group games facilitate communicative behaviour and share a number of common features. They:

- encourage peers to interact in meaningful activities;
- allow pupils to make decisions and have choices;

- encourage pupils to voice their opinions to peers;
- allow less able communicators to see good models of speaking and listening;
- develop general rather than specific goals, e.g. those stated on a Group Education Plan (GEP); and
- develop skills of social interaction which spill over into all areas of the curriculum.

Whatever their targets, the majority of children benefit from group activities and games.

1. Turn-taking games – most reading and spelling games can develop turn-taking skills at the same time as they develop literacy. Snap, pairs, happy families, dominoes and so on are all games which rely on waiting for a turn. Behavioural rewards could actively encourage the social element.
2. Active listening – this activity focuses on listening, and reminds the group who is speaking. Throw a small, soft ball for the speaker to hold, and throw the ball to the next person who puts up their hand to speak (on any agreed topic). Children with poor communication often need reminding of the roles of speaker and listener.
3. Opinions – many pupils struggle to express their opinions and feelings verbally. Group discussion can be initiated by a statement or a stimulus of some kind. Pupils can indicate their likes or dislikes by holding up a card stating 'I like that' or 'I don't like that'. Pupils can elaborate on their choice verbally, and expand on their reasons if they wish to.
4. Asking questions – set up interview situations by inviting a person to join the group and be interviewed. Children have responded well to interviewing the caretaker, secretary, a teacher, or a younger/older child. Interviews can relate to topics, e.g. interviewing a person about life in the thirties.

   Question-asking is a difficult task for a child with low esteem and poor language levels. Some pupils may have to go through a number of preparatory stages before they can ask questions with confidence. For example, they may repeat questions already asked by teacher or peers; choose a question from a given list; prepare questions first, with support, ready to ask later; prepare their own questions for interview; match questions to the interviewee (e.g. to the school cook, 'What kind of cooking do you like best?') and, finally, pupils join in spontaneous questions and answers in a range of settings.
5. Instructions – games can involve pupils in:
   - giving each other instructions, e.g. to select from an assortment of objects on a table; or
   - instructions of direction/movement, e.g. left or right.
6. Description – group games can arise from assorted pictures or objects on a table. As each one is described (by adult or pupil) others in the group can 'claim' it, from its description. Pupils can take turns to describe the objects.
7. Focusing on details – small, hand-size telephones make a useful prop. Children in a group take turns to talk to a partner 'on the telephone' with their eyes closed, e.g. about their weekend news. The aim is to focus on language details without accompanying gesture.

All pupils benefit from explicit feedback about their communication, precise modelling, and opportunities to practice with different mixes and sizes of groups.

Collaborative work with ICT

Work on the computer can help to develop through talk the social skills of children with special educational needs. Brooks (1997) describes a number of case studies from her research into effective strategies for using ICT in mainstream schools.

Jake had delayed communication skills, and was usually paired on the computer with Kevin, who talked a lot and made a good role model. Jake was more talkative when working on the computer than at any other time. He explained to other pupils how to use the 'talking dictionary' CD-ROM, discussed which icons to click, and read aloud some of the names from the screen. Jake's teacher stated that when sat at his desk he interacted far less with other pupils.

An alternative example from this research describes Patrick, who has cerebral palsy. Patrick relied on ICT for his written work. In one observed lesson, Patrick was the scribe for his group, and entered onto his computer data about shoe sizes. This was seen as an advantage by members of the group and helped to counteract Patrick's isolation when he had to use the computer by himself.

The computer supports collaborative work on language and social skills, as well as work on literacy and numeracy.

Talk through DARTS activities

Talk helps to develop reading, and is itself developed through the activities themselves. Directed activities related to texts (DARTS) refers to any activity which focuses on a specific aspect of reading, e.g. extracting details from a text; working on sequence by arranging words into sentences, or sentences into a paragraph; or work on comparison, cause and effect and so on.

DARTS activities are a key feature of the literacy hour, as children work on identified NLS objectives during independent activities. Talk is a major part of the task, enabling children to develop their reading skills at the same time as they develop their speaking and listening skills.

This chapter has focused on activities designed to develop language and communication skills through class or group work. Organising practical activities effectively depends on efficient use of resources. This will be discussed in the following chapter.

Chapter 9

Using Resources Effectively

In the context of this book resources includes people as well as materials. This chapter considers how human and material resources support language and communication difficulties.

Utilising human resources

For human resources to be used effectively, there must be shared understanding of which staff support particular areas of learning difficulty. Figure 9.1 lists a range of adults, in and outside the school, any of whom could support children with speaking and listening difficulties at any time.

In the school	External specialists/voluntary helpers
Head teacher	SEN specialist teachers
Subject leader	Bilingual support teacher
SENCO	Visual impairment specialist
SEN governor	Hearing impairment specialist
Literacy coordinator	Speech and language therapist
Literacy governor	Teacher for behaviour support
Numeracy coordinator	Educational psychologist
Class teacher	Teacher for the support of children with physical disabilities
Subject specialist	
Learning support assistant (LSA)	Support teacher for traveller pupils
	Parents
	Voluntary helpers

Figure 9.1 Adults in and outside the school

During a typical week, the class teacher will be involved with language most of the time. The SENCO and literacy or numeracy coordinators may meet to discuss key issues to do with NLS or NNS policy and practice. External specialists make routine visits to support staff and pupils. Parents or voluntary helpers are employed around the school, often working with groups in classrooms. The educational psychologist may assess a child or offer advice, and the head teacher and governors, if not directly involved, make available the resources needed. In a large school the number of staff interacting with each other on aspects of SEN is considerable.

Roles and responsibilities

Who has responsibility for language and communication? It could be argued that as speaking and listening permeates the whole curriculum, everyone in the school is responsible for its development, if only to provide consistent role models. A school with clear internal roles and responsibilities is more likely to use external support to advantage. In a small school one person may wear a number of hats. In a large school, roles often overlap, but who would have overall responsibility for:

- training school staff in how to differentiate questioning?
- running a parents workshop on communication skills?

- liaising with the speech and language therapist?
- organising language activities to be done by LSA staff?
- organising voluntary helpers for language work?
- liaising with the educational psychologist?
- discussing how children with language difficulties have progressed in the literacy hour with the external SEN specialist who supports it?
- discussing children's vocabulary in the numeracy hour?

There are no right answers. If human resources are to be maximised, all internal and external adults have to know their role, and how it interacts with that of others.

Support through the IEP

Any child with difficulties in speaking and listening should have an IEP, and be identified on the SEN Code of Practice (DfE 1994) at an appropriate stage. Such children may also have literacy and/or numeracy difficulties. A child with significant language and communication difficulties may well have a statement of SEN which specifies additional support to be provided by the LEA.

The most effective means of organising support for all learning difficulties, including language and communication, is through IEP and annual review meetings, which act as staging points through which relevant human resources are identified and support strategies actioned. An effective IEP will include clear statements on the pupil's learning targets, how the school will help him to achieve them, and which resources are to be used (i.e. human and material).

If all adults involved in a child's support have a copy of the IEP, coordination is half-way there. The IEP should state clearly what each person will do to support the child: what will the school staff do? what will external specialists do? how will parents or voluntary adults help?

The LSA

This section looks at how the LSA can support speaking and listening, and the conditions which help to make LSA support effective. The following questions should be asked:

- what is the purpose of LSA support and who is actually to receive it – individual children, identified groups or the class in general (e.g. during the literacy hour)?
- is the LSA to support in the classroom or by withdrawal?
- what does the LSA need to know in order to perform his or her role?

Depending on the purpose of the LSA, information provided may need to include:

- names of children and their particular difficulties;
- the NLS or NNS objectives being taught so that the LSA can see how the child's IEP targets relate to the main learning objectives;
- strategies for working with the target areas, e.g. for language, the LSA needs to know how to develop the areas of language, and how to analyse the child's responses;
- which materials to use and how to use them;
- what records are to be kept and where they are to be stored ready for use at the next IEP or annual review; and
- who to register concerns to or liaise with.

Whether the LSA supports the literacy or the numeracy hour, or works with groups of pupils at other times, he or she needs to know how to differentiate questions, and to give instructions at an appropriate level for the children being supported.

Case studies

For children with significant language and communication difficulties, the LSA is often the main resource to help with the child's difficulties. The weekly hours of additional support could be considerable.

Case study 1 – Emma

Emma is a Year 1 pupil with a statement for language and communication difficulties. LSA support is assigned to address significant language delay, and to work with Emma for one and a half hours daily. The speech and language therapist has provided a programme of objectives for the LSA to work on, and the SENCO has discussed with the LSA how to address these and which resources to use. Figure 9.2 shows the language targets identified for Emma.

Areas of language to be developed:

1. Verbs and prepositions.
2. Words of colour, size and shape.
3. Vocabulary of clothing.
4. Vocabulary of the emotions.

Emma's targets to be achieved by the next IEP (broken down from the Annual Review):

1. To listen and respond to single step instructions;
2. To produce 'three word' utterances, including the vocabulary listed (e.g. the red jumper);
3. To express own needs and feelings;
4. To demonstrate the above skills across the curriculum.

Figure 9.2 Emma's language and communication targets

Emma's support programme raises a number of key issues:

- focused support needs to be frequent, often daily. How can this be integrated with the literacy or numeracy hours?
- Emma's achievements should be assessed in and out of the classroom. If the LSA is to work individually on the targets, how is Emma's progress in class to be monitored?

Case study 2 – Alex

Alex is a Year 8 pupil, but the issues arising from his case study could easily apply to pupils at Key Stage 2. Alex has a statement for severe and specific memory and language difficulties. Alex's receptive language skills are better developed than his expressive language skills. He has difficulty ordering ideas, using syntax, planning speech and finding words he wants to use, he is unable to remember letters, sounds and numbers, and has difficulty in areas of literacy and numeracy. Figure 9.3 lists the targets identified for Alex at his last annual review meeting, which are expressed as pupil outcomes in context.

Alex has an LSA assigned for 16 hours per week, because his statement is for significant language and communication difficulties. The LSA supports Alex in various subjects of the curriculum because Alex has expressed his wish not to be withdrawn from the classroom.

Both pupils receive support from an LSA, yet the allocation of time varies. Emma's support is focused towards specific areas of vocabulary at an early level of language acquisition, i.e. three-word utterances. Alex, by Year 8, speaks in sentences and has acquired a basic level of language competency, with a vocabulary of common words, but needs support to develop his understanding and use of core subject vocabulary, to develop word finding skills, and to function more effectively as a member of a group.

Alex
In all subjects:
1. Extend understanding of subject vocabulary;
2. Contribute to small group discussion;
3. Ask questions during group activities;
4. Speak to group about a range of topics using acquired vocabulary.

Figure 9.3 Alex's targets

The LSA is a crucial part of the support programme for these pupils and others with broadly similar needs. One key issue for the SENCO in Alex's school was how best to use the considerable amount of LSA time allocated to Alex. In this particular case, the LSA played a key role in the classroom, supporting group work and observing the language skills Alex demonstrated. The situation was helped by Alex being allowed to indicate in which subject he needed most support.

LSA training

If LSAs are to perform their role independently they need to be trained in language and communication skills, as well as in areas of SEN. The LSA supporting Emma needs to know how language develops and what to observe; different levels of instructions; and methods and approaches for developing language. The LSA supporting Alex needs to know the core vocabulary for each subject area; how to observe Alex's use of language in a small group; and how to recognise Alex's needs and be able to prompt as necessary, yet unobtrusively to avoid embarrassment.

All LSAs need basic training in SEN (for example the Code of Practice, DfE 1994), how to work with IEPs, strategies and resources and how to maintain effective and useful records. The Teacher Training Agency (1998) has pledged to increase training opportunities for all specialist SEN staff, having recognised their major role in all areas of learning.

The external specialist teacher

Many children have language difficulties which are not significant enough to require speech or language therapy. Their needs may be met by a teacher from the LEA Special Educational Need Support Service, addressing the pupil's IEP targets in negotiation with the school. SEN specialist teachers often allocate an amount of time each week to support a school, and may directly teach children at Stage 3 of the SEN Code of Practice. SEN support teachers may also work with children who have statements for learning difficulties, which may include some form of language delay.

Support teachers may work in the classroom, or withdraw children to work individually, in pairs, or in groups. Ainscow and Florek (1989), with reference to in-class support, comment that 'schools tend to set up initiatives to support children with SEN within the ordinary classroom before they have fully considered the issues, implications, and conditions crucial to success.' Negotiation at the start of the period of support, and continued liaison with key school staff and the support teacher throughout, is essential, yet lack of time is often expressed as a problem.

Support staff may address any area of SEN. In this section, pupils with language and/or literacy difficulties will be considered, along with the issues which will need to be negotiated before the support begins. Having identified the purpose of the support, and the pupil(s) to be supported, schools need to liaise on the following issues.

1. Time – if a specialist teacher has only one day per week in a school to support identified school issues, and some children are at Stage 3 of the Code, how is that time best used? What are the priorities of need? If the SEN teacher is to support a child with a statement, time for that is usually identified separately, in addition to the time allocated for non-statemented pupils. The statement is a legal document.
2. How is the support to be delivered? External specialists cannot always arrange a particular day or time. Often, these staff support a number of schools, and have to balance the needs of each. The decision to work out of the classroom, in the literacy or numeracy hour, or in another subject area, needs to be carefully made. What are the priorities within the practical constraints?
3. What are the expected outcomes from the SEN teacher's period of support? If the support teacher directly teaches a group of pupils in greatest need, should the language and literacy levels of those children show an increased rate of improvement by the end of the term or the year? Can such an improvement be directly attributable to the specialist teacher's intervention without other in-school factors being taken into account?

SEN specialist teachers are often included on the LEA's Educational Development Plan for improving school attainment in literacy and/or numeracy. SEN teams centrally managed by the LEA are additional human resources for the benefit of teaching and learning in schools (and sometimes pre-school establishments). If focused activities which include language are part of the child's programme, it is essential that progress is assessed both in and out of the classroom to ensure that skills are transferred into all lessons.

Case study 1 – Mark at Stage 5 of the Code

Mark is supported by a specialist SEN teacher for half an hour each week, and also attends a language unit. Mark has an individual programme with precise targets for language, literacy and numeracy. Mark's language programme has been integrated into the general programme provided by the SEN specialist teacher. His areas of progress include:

- improved ability to follow simple oral instructions;
- increased contribution to group discussion;
- appropriate use of question vocabulary;
- improved use of sequential concepts such as first, next; and
- improved social gestures, e.g. eye contact.

The SEN teacher supports Mark mainly out of the classroom, for half an hour each week, for integrated language and literacy activities. In addition, once every half-term, the SEN teacher tries to observe Mark in the classroom to see how he is transferring his skills into other lessons. Provided that Mark receives the equivalent of half an hour per week of focused time, the SEN specialist reserves some flexibility with her timetable in order to observe his language and communicative behaviour in different lessons where possible. Observing and recording Mark's language and communication (as well as literacy or numeracy) in the classroom allows her to monitor whether teaching has resulted in learning. The SEN teacher's classroom presence links what is taught during a withdrawn situation with its ultimate objective, i.e. its use in lessons, as Mark sees the same teacher in both contexts.

Case study 2 – Pupils at Stage 3 of the Code

The support time for this case study coincides with the literacy hour. The SEN specialist teacher, SENCO and class teachers have negotiated support in the classroom for the two available mornings of the week.

The objectives of the SEN support are:

- to monitor the progress of Stage 3 pupils in listening, speaking, reading and writing, in the classroom context, focusing on Key Stage 1, for the duration of the term;
- to work with the relevant class teachers in developing effective strategies for engaging all pupils in whole-class work, and meeting the range of needs; and
- to work with relevant class teachers in developing the effectiveness of independent activities for all children.

To facilitate these objectives, negotiated strategies include:

- focusing on a group of Stage 3 pupils in the literacy hour for two mornings per week, rotating this between different classrooms each half-term to cover each year group;
- monitoring whole-class interaction, and observing how particular pupils are responding;
- observing independent activities and helping to develop strategies and resources which develop NLS objectives yet enable pupils to be self-reliant; and
- using other parts of the morning, where possible, to cultivate talk in other subject areas.

How does this type of support enhance pupils' speaking and listening skills? Two teachers in one classroom provide increased opportunities for both staff to observe different children and the extent of their learning. Throughout this process of exploration, much evaluative discussion can take place on what both teachers have observed through their team approach. The following observations were made during evaluative discussion between teachers:

- more able pupils needed to be stretched during their independent activities;
- a visually impaired (VI) child needed to be seated differently;
- a group of quiet children who rarely joined in whole class discussion were not engaging with general questions and needed questions aimed directly at them to keep them alert.

This support also stimulated discussion between school staff and the SEN specialist teacher on how children with SEN were included in the literacy hour through interactive talk. The support included a whole staff training workshop on differentiated questioning, sharing with staff the strategies jointly devised by class teachers and the SEN teacher.

The point of these case studies is to illustrate various ways in which SEN specialist teachers can support language and communication, through focused activities, in-class support, or a mixture of both. The role should be whatever is negotiated between school and specialist teacher.

Bearn and Smith (1998), from a study of the support teacher role, identified some ideal roles as suggested by teachers themselves: 'carer, consultant, assistant teacher, expert, mediator, calming influence, enabler, partner and someone who differentiates resources'. Whatever the actual roles in relation to the ideals, specialist teachers working in and out of the classroom can promote integrated teaching and learning through teamwork. As Ainscow and Florek (1989) further commented, 'two in harmonious collaboration add up to more than the sum of one and one.'

Speech and language therapy service

The role of the speech and language therapist is described by Wagge (1989) as being concerned with the development of communication. Speech and language therapists assess, plan and implement strategies in every area of speech and language with children whose skills are delayed, or who may have lost their abilities through illness or trauma. Speech and language therapy services are for children of all ages, from birth, take place in a variety of settings and are managed largely through NHS trusts.

Meeting Special Educational Needs: A Programme of Action (DfEE 1998a), the government's revised document following responses to the original Green Paper, pledges to improve the provision of speech and language therapy through more effective partnerships between NHS trusts and education.

How do speech and language therapy services work with schools? Jowett and Evans (1996) have identified much diverse practice in the delivery of speech and language therapy. While collaboration is seen as important, their research points to key differences in how teachers and therapists view their respective roles. Teachers work from an educational model, with an overview of the whole curriculum, while therapists work within a medical model, planning their own remediation programmes focused on communication objectives.

Differences in perspective are easily integrated: communication is cross-curricular. The LSA often follows a programme devised by the therapist, in the context of education. Collaboration needs to include the LSA as the link between teacher, therapist and other SEN staff, e.g. the SENCO.

The research identified training for teachers and LSAs. In one LEA, training courses were delivered over two days for teachers, and separate courses over three days for LSA staff. Training began with an overview of communication, followed by sessions on verbal comprehension, expressive language, the use of language and speech clarity. Part of the feedback included comments that the input had 'raised the quality of the work with all children, particularly those with language problems'. One issue concerning speech and language therapy is that the medical model reiterates a clinic-based service that is isolated from the education children receive. The government's partnership pledge recognises the need for:

- therapists to work in schools to show staff how specific speech and language activities should be done;
- therapists to observe children in the classroom;
- programmes which match the child's abilities to the educational context, e.g. the child may be advised by the therapist to write something down, but be unable to write; and
- joint ownership of speech and language programmes.

Supporting the sensory impaired child

Services for sensory impaired children are normally managed by the LEA. Enlisting support from the relevant service could make the difference between a hearing (HI) or visually impaired (VI) child accessing the literacy and numeracy hours or not. Specialist equipment may be necessary to overcome the access barrier and enable speaking and listening for all children.

Specialist teachers from the services for sensory impairment may work in the classroom in order to:

- analyse classroom conditions and work with the class teacher to facilitate effective communication;
- monitor the child's communication in the classroom; or
- check equipment (e.g. hearing and vision aids).

LSA staff play a key role in enabling access to the literacy and numeracy hours for children with sensory impairment by:

- taking notes for them during whole-class work;
- introducing them to big books before the session where possible, e.g. during a weekly preparation session;
- listing new vocabulary in a glossary for later work; and
- supporting the integration of sensory impaired children into group work by a discrete presence.

Supporting the child with challenging behaviour

Many general strategies, e.g. differentiated questioning, can reduce challenging behaviour; but some children may need a behaviour plan which focuses on communicative strategies in the classroom or in the playground, drawn up with the support of a teacher specialising in behaviour.

A whole-school policy for speaking and listening will effectively deal with many potential discipline problems by stating clearly boundaries, rules and procedures; and teaching children from the start of education how to behave to whom, where, and when.

Challenging behaviour is reduced when children are explicitly taught how to communicate through language:

- to different people – head teacher, teaching and non-teaching staff, caretaker, peers, younger children, visitors; and
- in different settings – during class teaching, as group members, along the corridor, entering assembly and so on.

The above strategies could address communication issues centred around expected standards of behaviour, but children whose challenging behaviour stems from emotional difficulties may need more specialised support from an educational psychologist, as well as a behaviour specialist.

Training in SEN specialisms

The Teacher Training Agency (1998) has identified 'speech, language and communication difficulties' as one of the nine SEN specialisms on which to focus training, the aim being to achieve national standards for staff specialising in certain areas of SEN. Interestingly, the document does not list 'moderate learning difficulties' as an SEN specialism in its own right. The document states that, 'In reality, pupils with general learning difficulties are increasingly supported in mainstream schools.' Many children presently identified as having moderate learning difficulties (MLD) also have language and communication problems which are expected to be addressed through the routines of the classroom. Many of the strategies explored in this book support that aim.

The nine areas of SEN identified for specialist training involve communication, each from a different perspective. The SEN specialisms are autism, emotional and behavioural difficulties, deafness, deaf-blindness, physical disabilities, severe and profound learning difficulties, specific learning difficulties, visual impairment, and speech, language and communication difficulties.

Many children whose difficulties fall within the above categories progress in mainstream schools with appropriate provision and additional human resources. The extent to which they progress depends on the training allocated, not only to SEN specialist teachers, but to class teachers and LSAs, who enable inclusion to work effectively for all children, including those without SEN.
The main point of this section is that language and communication enables learning for all children, and will form a large part of the training delivered to those specialising in the SEN areas listed. Combining basic classroom strategies for developing speaking and listening with the SEN specialist knowledge available is the most effective way to maximise human resources.

Parents

The DfEE programme of action on SEN (DfEE 1998a) devotes the first of its five chapters to 'working with parents to achieve excellence for all', emphasising the crucial role of parental support for all children. Developing family literacy is a priority, since most involvement with parents, in school or at home, focuses on areas of literacy and numeracy. Parents may support their own child or other children by:

- involvement in the literacy (or numeracy hour);
- listening to children reading;
- working with writing groups;
- parental workshops, often for children with SEN;
- helping to prepare resources;
- helping with homework; and
- supporting their child's IEP targets.

Language and communication skills are a central feature of parental support, yet talk rarely features on the agenda for parental involvement. To support the development of speaking and listening skills, parents and voluntary helpers need to understand how talk enables all learning; talk as part of reading and writing; and the role of talk in maths and other subjects.

If children's attitudes to talk are to improve, parents need to perceive speaking and listening as valuable activities in their own right and to promote that perception. Specifically, the parents of children with language and communication difficulties (and other learning difficulties) need to know:

- the nature of their child's difficulty;
- what is being done to address it;
- the key person to speak to about it;
- any external professionals supporting their child, e.g. the speech and language therapist; and
- what they or other voluntary helpers can do to help.

Training parents and voluntary helpers

All adults supporting learning need to work independently if their value as human resources is to be realised. Training parents and voluntary helpers to support language and communication has many benefits. Training could include:

- teaching on the role of talk in all areas of learning;
- how to develop their child's effective listening;
- how to enhance their child's speaking by sensitively adding (with reference to Manolsen 1992) to what is said;
- how to develop language through play;
- the language needed as a child moves through education, e.g. main words from the reading scheme, subject vocabulary at every key stage; and
- information on their child's particular problem area and their part in addressing the difficulties.

Most attention is focused on the parents of young children and the role of language during early years, but the value of the parental role is experienced at every key stage, not least at secondary level. Consider the following examples:

1. At the dentist's surgery, I watched a mother playing with her daughter in the waiting room. The focus of the talk was a set of six plastic animals, two of each colour, each slotting together. With that single toy, the potential for concept development was vast, for example:
   - numbers/counting – how many animals? How many of each animal?
   - colours – what colour are the dogs? How many rabbits are blue?
   - categorisation and sets – how many animals are pink and yellow? Let's make a set of blue, or pink and yellow?
   - order and prepositions – shall we put the yellow dogs at the front/back? What colour is the third one?

The potential, especially in the home environment, was significant, even with one small toy. This kind of work is the feature of the portage service (see next section).

2. Consider a child still struggling to develop language at Year 6, or later, when subject vocabulary has become a central feature of cross-curricular learning. In this context, the parent or voluntary helper could play a key role in talking about subject words, through homework or as part of a specific contribution to the child's IEP. Time is short in school and talk is often left out, not because it is seen as unimportant, but because reading and writing often play a more central role and provide evidence of what has been done.
3. Home visits provide a pivot around which focused support revolves. A half-hour session talking about the importance of talk in the home, showing parents how to use playthings and objects to develop language, often works wonders.
4. Parental workshops in school, or after school, for groups of parents at any key stage, could effectively train parents in maths or literacy talk, or how to develop children's effectiveness as members of a group.

Rarely is training for parents and voluntary helpers high on the staff development agenda, yet all adults need to know what they are doing and how to do it if their potential as a human resource is not to be wasted. Opportunities could be found during assemblies, as part of parents' evenings and at other key functions. Such time is well spent if independent and well-trained adult helpers are the result.

Portage

Portage exists as a pre-school service, normally managed by an LEA, for the support of children with SEN and their families. Children who receive portage support often have significant SEN which are apparent from birth or soon afterwards. Referral to the portage service may be through any professional involved with the pre-school child or through parents themselves.

A key feature of portage is its emphasis on early language and communication skills. Children with significant language delay are placed on a small-step programme based on the portage language checklist. The service aims to teach parents how to play and talk with their child, in accordance with the nature of their child's SEN.

While portage intervention is likely to cease as soon as a child attends an educational establishment, the objectives and strategies used by the portage service provide a useful reference point for schools and nurseries. Portage staff may operate a link support service for staff in LEA pre-school establishments so that a child's language and communication programme can be effectively continued.

The child

No exploration of human resources would be complete without reference to the learner. The government has pledged to strengthen the key part played by the child in his own development. *Meeting Special Educational Needs: A Programme of Action* (DfEE 1998a), states, 'We will strengthen the guidance in the Code (of Practice) to encourage LEAs and schools to seek and take account of the child's views throughout the SEN process.' Learners who know where they are going and how to get there will arrive sooner. As far as age and maturity allows, children need to be included at IEP review meetings and encouraged to play a role in their own assessment.

Many of the areas of training suggested for parents can be focused towards children's involvement in their learning, e.g. the value of talk. All children should know their learning goals and how to achieve them. Children with SEN, including language and communication difficulties, should be made aware of the significance of their IEP review meeting as the staging point for an assessment of their progress, and be involved in the decision-making arising from the meeting.

Using material resources

Resources for speaking and listening are less likely to feature on school capitation expenditure than those for other areas of learning, but reflection on resources for language and communication will highlight a few necessities.

Time in the literacy and numeracy hours

During the literacy hour, time is harnessed to the objectives of reading and writing. This book has emphasised the central role of talk in most activities which aim to raise standards in literacy. When time is short, do children write something down or talk about it? During the numeracy hour, do children work silently on paper or explain the answer to a problem to an adult or peer? Time is a consumable resource like any other and, given the crucial role of listening and speaking in literacy and numeracy, time for talk is essential.

Books read aloud

To encourage sharp listening skills, thought needs to be given to books which are read aloud at story time, or used for literature work with older children. Hoffman (1998) identified a number of key features to bear in mind when choosing books to read aloud to children of various ages, for example:

- repetition – the key feature of nursery rhymes and songs and a good way to reinforce vocabulary and encourage prediction skills;
- memorable words and phrases – to inspire children who need to develop fresh vocabulary;
- vivid characters – these will encourage children to tune in to the action, and will help to keep them all listening;
- another world to explore – to extend children's use of vocabulary and imagination;
- pictures and text which are well matched; and
- a satisfying ending – to enhance the impact of the book.

Repetition is a feature of many picture books and big books, reinforcing vocabulary and adding to the rhythm of the text. However, repetition is not synonymous with normal language and may confuse children who are not able to understand the literary style, e.g. 'she ran . . . and ran . . . and ran'. A common miscue when reading aloud is for children to repeat a word or phrase which is not repeated in the text. Talking about the reasons for repetition may help to prevent children with language difficulties from receiving the wrong message.

Books for reading to older children may have less repetition, fewer pictures and more characters, but still need to possess the other above qualities. Books for reading aloud do not have to be fiction; if reading aloud is to hook all listeners, non-fiction is more likely to interest boys. Choices which stem from the enthusiasm of an individual are more likely to sustain interest. Part of literacy, and the study of literature, is being introduced to new books, including books which are different, even controversial. Books which inspire children to talk about them – their characters, emotions, unusual theme and so on are linking listening and speaking with reading and writing, through their memorable and exciting content.

For general language work

For language work to be effective; a little thought needs to go into the resources. Most schools use a mixture of purchased materials and collated no-cost items.

Purchased equipment

Many publishers have collections of materials for language development, mostly aimed at early years and Key Stage 1. How useful are they? In addition, what is used as the stimulus for older children with language difficulties?

Many language items can be bought separately, or as sets, e.g. 'Chatter box' from NES/Arnold, which includes cards for work on actions, adjectives, prepositions, body parts, nouns and tense sequencing. While these materials are nicely produced and inspiring for language learners, many card-type resources are relegated to the back of a cupboard if their use is not clearly communicated. LSAs often tell me they have little idea of what resources are available for their use with groups of pupils.

Staff need to be trained in what to do with resources and how to get the best from them. During a 'resource training day', all adults, including LSAs and voluntary helpers, can share ideas for using card materials. Activities with a set of 'opposites' cards included:

- playing pairs or snap focusing on the 'opposites' words;
- children drawing their own pictures to illustrate each concept (and contribute to assessment);
- focusing on the colours and shapes on each card; and
- placing the cards into categories, e.g. people, transport.

To be cost-effective, purchased materials should perform a range of functions according to different children's needs.

A collection of items

Collecting items for language work is something children can do by themselves with a little help from adults. The author has found the following items useful.

1. Assorted pictures – sort a range of pictures into alphabetical order. Back them onto card and laminate them for instant use. Alternatively, sort into categories – emotions, colours, the body, animals etc. A file of picture cards generates thousands of words and lends itself to many hours of stimulating language work. Pictures for language work need not be restricted to Key Stage 1. Older children with receptive or expressive language difficulties may need the stimulus of pictures, e.g. to learn subject vocabulary.
2. Objects – for children with learning difficulties objects help to strengthen the language learning experience.
3. Plays – NES/Arnold produce differentiated plays for Key Stage 2 children. The 'Act 1' set has reading ages from five to seven years; the 'Act 2' set has reading ages of seven to nine years.
4. Letters – different letters develop language and literacy at the same time. Wooden, plastic or coloured letters, and letters with slightly different fonts (which do not confuse), will strengthen letter knowledge through activities focused on sets (e.g. of letters with the same features).
5. Photographs and postcards – children of every age will love to bring items for the collection. Such resources lend themselves to all kinds of talk, with a cross-curricular purpose – how town or styles of dress have changed.
6. Old catalogues – pictures from old catalogues support many language activities (e.g. the clothes game explained later).
7. Assorted equipment – mathematical shapes in different colours and sizes, marbles, counters, dice and other equipment lend interest to all kinds of

language work (e.g. the dice game explained later). A 'washing line' with 'clothes pegs' (example in Figure 9.4) can be used to illustrate almost any sequential concept and stimulates accompanying talk. 'Washing line talk' can be differentiated by pupils adding cards to the line at their own level and talking about their place in the sequence. On a 'fractions, decimals and percentages' line, some pupils may work in halves, while others demonstrate knowledge of hundredths and percentages, depending on their understanding.

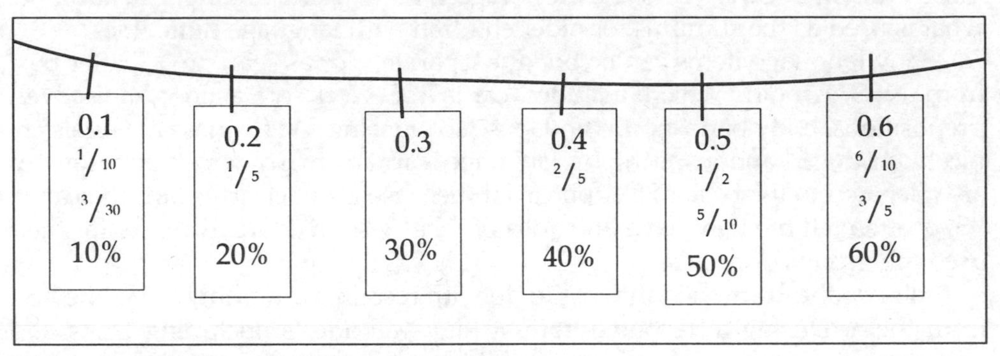

Figure 9.4 The 'washing line' sequence

Reading, writing and maths games

Many literacy and numeracy games also develop communication skills, e.g. turn-taking. Unleashed, the power of group work is immense. During a literacy training session, a group of teachers were using big books to plan literacy hours for the week. Ideas bounced between members of each group, projecting their thoughts from the 'what if' of the last comment. Thinking and language drove group momentum. The trainer wandered around at intervals (as a teacher would), maintaining focus on the task (the groups were finding it hilarious). Noise levels were high but the intended learning was very much in evidence.

Does this sound familiar? The groups could be children of any age, and learning could be focused on any aspect of literacy or numeracy, as well as other subjects. Through talk with lots of laughter, children develop communication skills, provided they can participate fully as group members.

While nothing can take the place of LSA training, LDA have produced briefing resource cards to assist LSAs working with Reception and Year 1 children. The 50 cards contain ideas for speaking and listening, e.g. listening attentively, following instructions etc., as well as reading and writing.

Resources for focused language work

For children who need activities aimed at specific areas of language and its functions, the following games illustrate how simple, low-cost resources can be used creatively.

1. Naming game with dice – use large dice to have fun with language work on naming, e.g. colours. A group game is played using dice with different coloured labels on each face. Children throw the die in turn, and name the colour to gain a point. Two dice could be used to play with colour and number. As both dice are thrown the child gains two points for saying both number and colour.
2. Description with cards – have children cut out pictures from old catalogues, and stick them onto card. Play the game by spreading the cards on the table so that all members can see them, e.g. cards showing clothes. Describe a card slowly, one attribute at a time ('A skirt . . . red and long') until a pupil recognises the description and claims the card. Repeat the descriptions until all cards are claimed. The child with most cards is the winner. Children could take turns to describe.

3. Categorisation with picture cards – use the same cards as above to focus on categorisation. Have individuals or pairs within a group collect pictures in sets following the principle of the happy families game. A child has to find a name for his set, e.g. people, animals, clothes.

A balance of simple, low-cost materials can have a range of uses according to children's language needs. The language objective needs to lead the materials used to achieve it.

Resources to enhance communication

Some resources that enhance access to speaking and listening activities are purchased from SEN statement funding and are used mainly to address specified needs. Specialist resources are also available from services, e.g. sensory impairment or physical disabilities services. Examples of resources are given below.

1. TEACCH – supports pupils with autism as well as other language and communication difficulties. As Jordan (1998) states, 'TEACCH . . . is an example of a good compensatory approach . . . based on a thorough and research-led understanding of . . . producing a prosthetic environment that accommodates the autistic style of thinking.'
2. ICT – many software programs intended to develop literacy or numeracy enhance speaking and listening skills. Some focus on words and meanings; the 'confusing words' series deals with English words which sound the same but are spelt differently, e.g. 'allowed' and 'aloud', 'its' and 'it's', 'your' and 'you're'.

   Software for ICT also incorporates talking pictures, many of which stretch to Key Stage 2, and a range of talking stories, which include some from the Oxford Reading Tree up to Level 3A. For Key Stages 2 and 3, 'ridiculous rhymes' help to develop rhyming skills, and may bring poetry to life for the disaffected.
3. Circle time poems – the principles can be adapted to suit a variety of situations. Circle time poems (NES/Arnold) are designed to link literacy with the emotions. They can be used in the literacy hour and during circle time to discuss children's personal responses to the issues raised, e.g. friendship, sharing, bullying.

This chapter has emphasised the effective use of human and material resources for a range of activities. Resources which develop language and communication rely on a careful assessment and recording of children's speaking and listening.

Chapter 10

Assessing and Recording Speaking and Listening

With time a constant problem, the most effective way to assess speaking and listening is through the context in which children are using language to communicate. The assessment of talk can also be used to assess progress in other areas of learning. This chapter explores the assessment of talk itself, the uses of talk to assess reading and writing, and the uses of talk to assess cross-curricular learning.

Talk should be observed from a range of contexts in which it happens. For children with language and communication difficulties, attempts to assess their skills through forced situations are unlikely to produce an accurate profile.

Talk from a broad evidence base

Evidence of children's speaking and listening skills can arise anywhere, but it would be impractical to assess the huge amount of children's talk that goes on every day. Consider the talk that takes place: as children come into school, in the cloakroom, during group work in the literacy hour, during whole-class work in the numeracy session, during pair work in a subject-based lesson, in the play ground, walking along the corridors, in PE, at the lunch table and communicating the choice of lunch.

Without a clear purpose, assessment would have no focus. What would we be looking for?

Why assess talk?

The main aim is to raise standards in learning. The objectives behind the assessment may vary, for example:

- to obtain a general profile of speaking and listening in order to assess each pupil's National Curriculum attainment level;
- to obtain a broad profile and plan an intervention programme for children who need it;
- to monitor the success of a language and communication programme already in place; or
- to assess and monitor the role of talk for other purposes, e.g. school-based research.

In practice, the above aims interact as purposes for assessing talk. Part of the assessment is to monitor general learning for all children, i.e. what they know about the uses of talk. Assessment also needs to uncover what particular children do not know and are not doing. Analysing reasons for assessment will identify which talk situations are to be observed and recorded.

Staging points for assessment

Assessment of talk (alongside that of reading and writing) needs to be an integral part of the teaching and learning cycle. If assessment is to achieve its purpose the process must be manageable and efficient. The following sections consider assessment in three stages — continuous, cumulative and summative.

Continuous assessment

Continuous assessment uses children's ongoing responses to teaching as evidence of learning. How do we know which talk is significant enough to be assessed? A general profile of children's talk from a range of contexts may need to be obtained. In this case, observation would include speaking and listening across a range of lessons, using whole-class, group and pair situations, as well as out-of-lesson contexts, e.g. at lunch and in the playground. Different groups could be observed in rotation.

If the purpose is to assess the language and communication of specific groups or individuals, e.g. to assess targets stated on an IEP (or GEP), the timing may need to be planned. If turn-taking is a target, either for a group or individuals, then group games may be the focus of observation. If answering questions during whole-class oral work is the target, then the first half-hour of the literacy or numeracy hour may provide a suitable context. If speaking in sentences or using standard English is the target area, then cross-curricular contexts could provide this evidence.

Continuous assessment also happens during the focused activities which are part of remediation programmes. If a child's target is to use prepositions correctly, his responses to focused teaching sessions on prepositions form part of that evidence, with other evidence of how prepositions are understood and used in other contexts.

Cumulative assessment

Continuous assessment collated and recorded on an ongoing basis informs the cumulative assessment needed for IEP or annual review meetings. If assessment has focused on specific targets, the continuous assessment records provide ready-made data to be summarised on a cumulative basis, e.g. each term.

Summative assessment

Cumulative assessment records almost write themselves into the summative records used for transition and for parental reports. Summative assessment should offer the next teacher and parents a summary of how speaking and listening skills have progressed for all children.

For children with no language and communication difficulties, the summative assessment may state in general terms their strengths and weaknesses. For children who are part of a GEP, or who have an IEP or a statement for SEN, the summative assessment should relate to identified targets.

Where does talk happen?

The following sections provide examples of where talk could be assessed as part of the three-stage process described above, focusing mainly on strategies for continuous assessment. When is talk assessed and where? How is talk assessed and by whom?

Assessing talk in the literacy hour

1. Assessment for this example stems from one of the NLS reading objectives for the week, i.e. pupils generating their own questions, and answering questions during whole-class work. The LSA is to observe different groups in rotation, focusing on one group each day during shared and word work. The teacher and LSA have devised a record sheet, as shown in Figure 10.1. The response sheet allows the LSA to note how a group of children respond to whole-class input, yet need not detract from focused support for a particular child with SEN.

RECORDING SHARED/WORD WORK						
Objective Questions **Group** Red **Date observed** 13/11/98						
Skills observed	AS	FG	RD	PR	TC	HS
Joined in shared text work	√	√	√		√	√
Response – general questions	√		√			
Response – direct questions	√	√	√		√	
Asked own questions	√		√		√	
Quality – literal					√	
inferential			√			
manipulative	√					

Figure 10.1 Responses to shared/word work in the literacy hour

2. During the literacy hour, the teacher assesses a group of children with poor communication skills whose target is to work effectively in pairs. As the teacher guides each group on a piece of writing, assessment of children's responses can take account of how each child in the group uses speaking and listening as part of the writing process. Later in the week, during the time for redrafting, the teacher goes around the classroom observing and recording how children work with a partner. Figure 10.2 illustrates how talk during pair-work could be recorded, focusing on different groups in rotation.

RECORDING PAIR WORK	
Name E. Howe **Class** 4R **Group** Swallows	
Skills observed	**Comments/notes**
Listened to partner's comments	Good eye contact, listened patiently
Responded politely to partner's comments.	Requested clarification from partner, made suggestions in light of what was said
Took note of comments and redrafted as necessary	Relooked at work with partner and amended some spellings, and vocabulary
Read partner's work evaluatively	Read it, but hesitant to make suggestions – needs confidence
Worked well with partner.	√ Polite and constructive

Figure 10.2 Recording talk during pair work

3. During independent activities, a group of children is playing dominoes. The activity uses word and picture cards, the objective being word recognition from the NLS Framework lists. The children have to match a word with its picture to complete the chain of dominoes. Figure 10.3 illustrates a group record sheet used to record both reading skills and the communication skills evident through the game.
4. A video produced by the Qualifications and Curriculum Authority (QCA) entitled *Gathering Evidence of Children's Reading Through Talk – Key Stage 1* (QCA 1998b) illustrates a range of contexts for assessing reading skills, which lead naturally to observation of how children use talk during the process. The examples do not address how data from talk can be recorded; memories of children's behaviour may not provide the accuracy required. Figure 10.4 illustrates a record for identifying reading behaviour and the talk that accompanies it. Continuous assessment emanates from normal teaching and learning activities and need not use additional time.

RECORDING GROUP WORK AND READING SKILLS		
Objective Word recognition	Group Circles	Date 6/12/98
Names of pupils	**Group behaviour observed**	**Reading skills observed**
A. Barnes	Awaited turn	Matched correct cards
S. Holt	Confused, kept forgetting when it was his turn	Needs to work on the first six words
B. Elliot	Took leadership role	Struggled to match words
P. Bell	Sullen and difficult, needs to establish group role	Needs more practice in these words
T. Stamp	Worked well with each group member	No problems. T. knows all these words

Figure 10.3 Group record for reading skills and talk

RECORDING READING AND RELATED TALK		
Name B. Holt	School Dean Year group 5	Date 6/2/99
Reading skills	**Comments**	**Use of language**
Recognised known words	Used his known words when reading science	Discussed the words he needs to learn next
Used phonic knowledge	Starting to use initial consonant clusters as strategies when reading	
Used context effectively	Still needs to focus on meaning — B. often ignores key clues.	
Used grammatical, graphic knowledge	Recognising main elements of words —ing, ed and using as strategies	
Demonstrated text comprehension	Responded well to inferential questions about history text	Answered in full sentences, with confidence, indicated understanding of vocabulary from the history text
Range of reading and attitudes	Still rather limited. Need to introduce more non-fiction texts — likes sports	

Figure 10.4 Recording reading and reading-related talk

Assessing talk in the numeracy session

1. Chapter 7 explored talk situations in maths which can be used to assess and record both areas of learning. If an LSA or other adult is available during the numeracy hour, whole-class work could be used to record talk and maths in the same way as in the previous section on literacy. Consider how the example in Figure 10.5 records a group's responses to mathematical activities.
2. A maths group working on problem-solving offers an opportunity to assess mathematical understanding and group dynamics at the same time, as illustrated in Figure 10.6.

MATHS RECORD FOR GROUP Topic Fractions	Group Blue	Date 13/6/98
Pupils	**Maths skills observed**	**Language use**
A. Holmes	Placed $^{3}/_{4}$ in correct place in line	Responded to general questions — explained why $^{2}/_{5}$ is same as $^{4}/_{10}$
S. Laker	Explained why $^{1}/_{5}$ equals 20%	Clear and confident. Used complete sentence
B. Waye	Held up $^{1}/_{5}$ as more than $^{1}/_{10}$ but could not say why	Reluctant to join in whole-class discussion — needs confidence

Figure 10.5 Recording responses in maths

MATHS GROUP ASSESSMENT Objective Problem-solving	Group Yellow	Date 5/3/98
Pupils	**Maths skills observed**	**Group dynamics**
A. Howe	Separated the problem into three steps — solved correctly	Group work well together and tend to support each other in solving problems. S. B. taking leadership role. P. L. needs to be more assertive.
P. Lomax	Struggled to understand the problem	
S. Bell	Transferred the problem to correct computation	
H. Driver	Confused — appeared not to understand the task	
P. Dean	Worked well — no difficulties	

Figure 10.6 Group assessment during maths

Cross-curricular observations

Subject talk offers opportunities for assessing speaking and listening. Consider the following activities and how each one offers opportunities for assessing talk and talk-related learning:

- art – working in pairs to mix paint colours to share;
- history – group work discussing primary and secondary sources of evidence;
- technology – making a group model. e.g. a Tudor house;
- drama – group work based on a social theme, e.g. bullying or friendship;
- geography - group work to collate and categorise pictures from different aspects of the environment, e.g. in the town or in the country; and
- computer work – to redraft writing in pairs.

Assessment of talk through the above areas, will depend on the objectives for each group or individual pupil and the contexts around which activities are based. The point is to reflect on how talk and subject learning can be assessed together, by observing the process (talk) as well as the product (completed piece of work).

Assessing talk through a reading or writing conference

Companion books by Edwards (1999a, b) refer to reading and writing conferences as cumulative assessment strategies. It is suggested that children have individual reading or writing conferences with the teacher every term, half-term, or as often as time allows. Part of the purpose of the conference, as well as to assess reading or writing, is for a child to enjoy quality time with the teacher and engage in meaningful and sincere one-to-one talk.

Cumulative assessment of literacy could also be used to assess the talk itself. Depending on the child's needs, the conference could offer an opportunity to:

- assess language in relation to a child's individual targets;
- assess the child's ability to talk about reading or writing, e.g. book language, vocabulary taught;
- assess the communication aspects of the interaction:
  —how well does he ask questions or initiate talk?
  —how well does he answer different kinds of questions (nod, one word, phrase, sentence)?
  —how accurately does he respond to teacher questions? and
- assess what the pupil thinks about his own learning, and talk sincerely about it.

The cumulative assessment conference could provide prime time for pupils who are otherwise shy or reluctant speakers to talk about themselves and their learning.

Where are records to be filed?

If continuous assessment uses different sources of evidence, material recorded should be efficiently organised. The following questions may help to suggest a policy.

1. For what purpose are individual records needed? If pupils have a loose-leaf file, separated into sections (language, reading, writing, maths etc.) records from a range of contexts and people are easily filed in it.
2. Do children each have a Record of Achievement (ROA) and is this separate from the individual file or part of it? If separate, what is the purpose of each?
3. In which contexts are group record sheets to be used, and by whom? Where are they to be filed for cumulative or summative use?
4. In which contexts are class record sheets to be used, and where are these to be filed?

Who assesses what and how?

Time rarely allows for talk assessment that is not combined with assessment of other learning. Talk assessment also needs to be shared between all the professionals involved, as well as with the child and his parents. The following sections offer suggestions for who might assess talk and how.

The child as an assessor

A key principle of this book, and the two companion books by Edwards (1999a, b) is the promotion of the ownership by all children of their own learning according to their age and level of maturity. The following strategies support that principle:

- all pupils could have their own speaking and listening goals stuck into their work files or exercise books;
- teach children to assess their own talk. Following a group discussion, use a few minutes to ask each child to assess his own use of talk, alone or in pairs. If children know how important talk is, and are prepared beforehand for their assessment role, they will respond in a mature way. Self-assessment could relate to children's goals; and
- show children how to sensitively assess each other's talk.

Teachers as assessors

If assessment is to be manageable, recording must be brief and instant, e.g. with pen and clipboard handy. Although it is suggested that assessment could focus on one group at a time, opportunities for assessing speaking and listening arise when they are least expected. Spontaneous notes on language as well as reading and writing could be made through the same task observation, as illustrated in Figure 10.7.

RECORD OF LANGUAGE, READING AND WRITING SKILLS		
Name H. Carson	**Class** 6R	
Date 16/4	**Task/activity** history dictionary	**Grouping** Red
Language	Made suggestions in group, voiced opinion, spoke clearly and managed to slow down.	
Reading	Demonstrated use of alphabetical roder, read the vocabulary cards unaided.	
Writing		
Date 17/5	**Task/activity** science	**Grouping** Blue
Language	Joined in discussion of experiment. Asked questions to clarify.	
Reading	Read instructions.	
Writing	Wrote report on experiment, as pair with A. B.	

Figure 10.7 Assessing language, reading and writing skills

The LSA as observer

LSAs often acquire a great deal of knowledge about children's strengths and weaknesses, and continuous records kept by LSAs should be used to inform the termly IEP or annual review meeting. Where LSAs are supporting the classroom in a general way, they are in a good position to observe all children's responses to teaching. LSAs often support the teaching, or the preparation of resources, but are not often shown how to support assessment and recording as part of a consistent, team-oriented approach.

If the records maintained are to be useful, LSAs need to know how to sift significant data from the mass of language and communication observed. A note on an LSA record that, 'John sat next to Sally in the group and played a game' may be significant if John has previously refused to sit next to, pair up with or communicate with, girls. If John is working towards a communication target of being able to work with girls (this is taken from a real case) such a comment is highly significant, and suggests a breakthrough towards achievement. Otherwise, the comment is of little use.

LSAs have the potential to support the assessment and recording process as part of a team, but need knowledge to perform the task. If recording children's responses from a group task, they need to know what the group objectives are, and what the individual objectives are within the group, e.g. for communicative behaviour.

To support the literacy hour or the numeracy session, the whole class may be working on independent behaviour as part of class-based language and communication targets. To support class-based targets the LSA needs:

- to know the targets – i.e. the pupil behaviour represented;
- to know how the observations are to be done, e.g. during independent activities focusing on one group at a time, or during whole-class delivery;
- a class or group record sheet according to the focus of the observations;
- training on how to record significant data; and
- to know where to file the records.

What are significant and useful comments on children's responses to teaching? Consider the following notes. Which ones tell us something about a child's speaking and listening skills and could form part of the cumulative summary for an IEP or annual review meeting?

- Anne completed Book 3;
- Pat asked three questions during whole-class discussion;
- John waited his turn when playing a game of snap;
- Helen worked well with the blue group;
- Carla compared a circle with a triangle stating three attributes of difference;
- Alan used good language;
- Alex answered questions using correct sentences;
- Barry used eye-contact during our focused session; or
- Elizabeth listened to the story all the way through.

Without the context, and the pupil's target, it may be difficult to decide which of the comments are useful or not. If Helen has a behaviour problem and does not normally work well with the blue group, then such a comment may be significant. 'Alan used good language' tells us little about the language used. Is the comment referring to vocabulary? Is it referring to sentence structure? The main point of this section is to highlight the potential for LSAs to support assessment and recording.

Parents' records

Parents can observe and record their child's use of language and communication in a context other than school. If a child with significant speech and language difficulties is working towards 'producing three word utterances' possibly including certain prepositions, adjectives of colour etc., whether he is achieving the target at home as well as in school is a highly significant factor. If a child's target is to 'listen for ten minutes to a story', that same target may also need to be reinforced at home.

Parents need to be informed about their child's targets for language and communication as well as for literacy or maths, and should be shown how to observe and record significant data. Parents also need to understand the importance of IEP and annual review meetings as cumulative staging points for discussing their child's progress. One way to encourage parents to record their child's language and communication is to include a column in the reading record book. According to the objective, parents could note:

- how their child talks generally about reading, as illustrated in Figure 10.8;
- how their child has responded to a specific target, e.g. listened to a story; and
- how their child has responded to a communication target, e.g. made a personal choice in a polite manner.

PARENTAL READING AND LANGUAGE RECORD		
Name of pupil A. Hart		School Dean Class 3B
Reading targets		**Language targets**
- Reads high-frequency words - Reads for meaning		- Discusses story with adult - Listens and responds to questions
Date	**Reading comments**	**Language comments**
13/5	Read well Confused 'when' and 'went'	Talked about story with me, and answered two questions on it.

Figure 10.8 Language and communication at home

If parents are assigned to help with one of their child's targets, as stated on the IEP or annual review document, the target(s) could be stated at the top of the column to encourage parents to observe it.

External specialist records

Any SEN external specialist involved with a child is there to support a learning difficulty. Part of that support involves keeping detailed records on the child's progress with reference to the specific targets the external specialist supports. The IEP or annual review document should state these targets. Good records should not require explanation. Record-keeping needs to partly resolve the difficulties of being unable to liaise with school staff as frequently as might be desired.

The following questions may stimulate thoughts on how records are to achieve their objective as useful and informative documents:

- where are continuous external records filed?
- in what form and when are they transferred or photocopied as a contribution to IEP and annual reviews?
- how do the records kept by external specialists link in with those of the class teacher, SENCO, LSA and parents?
- who coordinates them all?

Assessing bilingual learners

The Code of Practice (DfE 1994) emphasises the importance of the early identification of any form of SEN, and stresses that lack of competency in English is not to be equated with learning difficulties as understood by the Code. The Ethnic Minorities Support Services (1998), following a survey of Oldham primary and secondary schools, offer guidelines for assessing bilingual pupils in a range of developmental areas. For example, where specific weaknesses are noted in language development, e.g. poor listening or attention, poor verbal understanding or limited use of vocabulary, the following areas for consideration are suggested:

- are listening and speaking tasks 'context-embedded'? If they are, does this suggest specific vocabulary needs?
- do errors in spoken English occur where English language structure is dissimilar to mother tongue patterns?
- is the child being stimulated linguistically at home?
- is mother tongue development in line with age?
- is the pupil's sequence of language acquisition dissimilar to other pupils who have English as an additional language (EAL) and/or the pupil's siblings?

The booklet stresses the need for mother tongue assessment in order to give an accurate picture of general language development, which can then be compared with progress in the additional language. Language difficulties, while not in themselves indicative of a learning difficulty, often limit the pace of learning for any child, and may therefore lead to significant delays in literacy and other areas of learning which then emerge as learning difficulties.

Many of the strategies suggested for general assessment will help to identify bilingual learners whose use of English presents a cause of concern that is otherwise different from the need to simply acquire English. Once that cause for concern is registered, it is essential that a specialist from the bilingual support service is sought, so that a mother tongue assessment can identify specific needs, and a language programme can be initiated where necessary.

Baseline assessment

Schools are now required to administer baseline assessment for children in the Reception year. Performance Indicators in Primary Schools (PIPS) is one of a number of baseline tests which seek to obtain a profile of attainment starting with the knowledge and skills a child brings to the Reception year. The system monitors progress in main areas of education, including self-esteem.

PIPS offers two approaches to baseline assessment: the first fulfills SCAA criteria in its arrangements for pupils starting school, and the second provides a more comprehensive picture of progress during the first year. Over time, the data measures baseline attainment, i.e. the skills children bring to school, with the value-added attainment as they progress. Baseline assessment provides a starting platform for continued assessment of specified areas, including language and communication.

Baseline assessment provides a tool for measuring children's attainment and progress as individuals, and also indicates general learning trends and patterns.

Assessing through the desirable outcomes

Chapter 2 referred to the use of desirable outcomes as the broad objectives of pre-school education which lead on to the National Curriculum; but how are these to be recorded and assessed? A simple checklist from the desirable outcomes for language and literacy could form the basis of a speaking and listening record, as illustrated in Figure 10.9. Attainment over time could be indicated by dates, possibly in colour to indicate the rate of progress, if desired. The checklist is not intended to be prescriptive but can be adapted to suit differences in pre-school settings. Similar checklists could be devised to record desirable outcomes from the other areas of early learning and are of great help to Reception teachers. The checklist could also form the basis of assessment for older children with significant language delay.

RECORD OF EARLY SPEAKING AND LISTENING **Name** .... **Educational context**			
Language and literacy			
1. Speaks in single words Produces sentences		Speaks in phrases Speaks clearly	
2. Initiates conversation with peers Speaks in small group		Initiates conversation with adults Speaks in larger group	
3. Talks about events Sequences events		Tells story using pictures Invents own story	
4. Asks simple questions Uses appropriate words during pretend-play		Uses new words Conveys own ideas and opinions	
5. Listens to an adult Follows instructions Listens to rhymes Listens to partner		Listens to peers Responds to questions Listens to stories Listens in group	
6. Identifies common sounds e.g. bell Identifies sounds in own environment		Distinguishes between many sounds Describes range of sounds	

Figure 10.9 Assessing early speaking and listening

National feedback on talk

The Qualifications and Curriculum Authority (QCA) provides schools with useful data on national trends and patterns. One QCA report (QCA 1998d) discussed key features of writing across all key stages which have direct relevance to, and reflect, speaking and listening skills.

The report states that, 'Children in Key Stages 1 and 2 . . . use dialogue in their stories, but that dialogue rarely advances the plot or develops the characters. At Key Stage 3 children use dialogue infrequently in narrative writing . . .' Does this strengthen the argument that focused work on speaking could support the use of dialogue in writing? The same report further states that, 'More able children in Year 6 . . . use a wide range of sentence constructions . . . in complex sentences.' The report may be suggesting a less than desired use of sentence construction from the majority of pupils, and points out the need for focused work on sentences at all key stages.

A further QCA report (QCA 1998c) on Key Stage 1 national standards using 1997 data made reference to the teacher assessment of Attainment Target (AT) 1 in each of the core subjects. The data indicated that:

- more teachers reported their use of observations for assessing Experimental and Investigative Science than for Using and Applying Mathematics or for Speaking and Listening;
- more records are kept for the Science AT1 than for AT1 in Maths or English;
- teachers find it difficult to keep records for Speaking and Listening; and
- more than 50 per cent of the teachers said that they rely to some extent on their memory of a child's attainment when making judgements in Speaking and Listening and in Using and Applying Mathematics.

Sixty per cent of teachers in the sample reported that their decisions about the levels in these two attainment targets (AT1 in Maths and English) are ongoing throughout the Key Stage, although 36 per cent said they do not make any decisions until the end of the Key Stage.

The QCA data raise a number of issues, not least the difficulties in maintaining records for Speaking and Listening which provide:

- cumulative and summative data for all children, that is accurate and detailed; and
- a diagnostic profile of strengths and weaknesses to identify language and communication difficulties early and inform planning on an ongoing basis.

This chapter has explored a number of assessment and recording issues, and has offered suggestions for making systems manageable and informative. Effective assessment and recording depends on:

- brevity – write clearly but concisely;
- rotation – between particular groups as necessary;
- focus – relate observations to group or individual objectives;
- coordination – make records work by avoiding duplication, e.g. different people recording in different contexts;
- simplicity – so that children/parents can understand them;
- appropriateness – when are class, group or individual records best?
- sharing – of the load, and to create awareness of a child's progress by everyone involved; and
- efficiency of time-scale – matched to the three-stage system of continuous, cumulative and summative assessment.

One overriding point is that records need to be significant and relevant for their purpose and need to inform future planning, even by the next teacher. All children need to take turns in conversation, but the comment that 'John waited for his turn in a group game' is only relevant if John is working towards achieving that particular target. If John always awaits his turn, the comment is useless.

Language and communication are cross-curricular. This chapter has highlighted the importance of assessing speaking and listening skills using a broad evidence base, related to the normal activities of teaching and learning.

Conclusion

The theme of this book is the central role of talk as a foundation for all learning. For poor spellers, spell-checkers can help. Dictionaries are available to support reading and writing. Speaking and listening rely on human interaction to develop skills and strategies.

Teaching is not just telling or giving children information; teaching involves dialogue. Speaking and listening have the potential to turn lectures into a range of teaching and learning opportunities for all children.

Bibliography

Ainscow, M. and Florek, A. (1989) *Special Educational Needs: Towards a Whole School Approach* London: David Fulton Publishers.
Barnes, D., Britton, J. and Rosen, H. (1971) *Language, the Learner and the School.* Harmondsworth: Penguin.
BBC (1975) *2nd House.* Broadcast 2nd January 1975.
BBC TV (1998) *Numeracy in Action.* Broadcast on BBC2, 18th December 1998.
Beard, R. (1987) *Developing Reading 3 – 13.* London: Hodder and Stoughton.
Bearn, A. and Smith, C. (1998) 'How learning support is perceived by mainstream colleagues', *Support for Learning***13**(1).
Bell, D. (1998) 'Accessing science: challenges faced by teachers of children with learning difficulties in primary schools',*Support for Learning* **13**(1).
Brooks, R. (1997) *Special Educational Needs and Information Technology.* Slough: The National Foundation for Educational Research.
Brown, R. (1973) *A First Language: The Early Stages.* Harmondsworth: Penguin Books.
Browne, A. (1996) *Developing Language and Literacy 3 – 8.* London: Paul Chapman Publishing.
Bunting, R. (1997) *Teaching about Language in the Primary Years.* London: David Fulton Publishers (in association with the Roehampton Institute, London).
Carroll, L. (1962a) *Alice's Adventures in Wonderland.* London: The Folio Society.
Carroll, L. (1962b) *Through the Looking-Glass.* London: The Folio Society.
Connery, V. (1987) *Praxis Makes Perfect.* Hitchin, Herts: Dyspraxia Foundation.
Cox, T. (1996) *The National Curriculum and the Early Years.* London: Falmer Press.
DfE (1967) *The Plowden Report: Children and their Primary Schools: A Report of the Central Advisory Council for Education (England).* London: HMSO.
DfE (1975) *The Bullock Report: A Language for Life.* London: HMSO.
DfE (1994) *The Code of Practice for the Identification and Assessment of Special Educational Needs.* London: HMSO.
DfE (1995a) *English in the National Curriculum.* London: HMSO.
DfE (1995b) *Geography in the National Curriculum.* London: HMSO.
DfE (1995c) *History in the National Curriculum.* London: HMSO.
DfEE (1998a) *Meeting Special Educational Needs: A Programme of Action.* London: HSMO.
DfEE (1998b) *National Literacy Strategy: Framework for Teaching.* London: HMSO.
DfEE (1998c) *National Literacy Strategy, Training Module 6.* London: HMSO.
DfEE (1998d) *Numeracy Matters.* London: HMSO.
DfEE (1998e) *The Implementation of the National Numeracy Strategy.* London: HMSO.
DfEE/QCA (1998) *Supporting the Target Setting Process – Guidance for Effective Target Setting for Pupils with Special Educational Needs.* London: DfEE.
Edwards, S. (1999a) *Reading for All.* London: David Fulton Publishers.
Edwards, S. (1999b) *Writing for All.* London: David Fulton Publishers.
El-Naggar, O. (1994) *Differentiation Through Maths Trails.* Tamworth: NASEN.
Ethnic Minorities Support Services (1998) *Guidelines for the Assessment of Bilingual Pupils who may have Learning Difficulties.* Oldham Educational and Leisure Services: Oldham.
Golding, W. (1958) *Lord of the Flies.* London: Faber.

Grudgeon, E., Hubbard, L., Smith, C. and Dawes, L. (1998) *Teaching Speaking and Listening in the Primary School.* London: David Fulton Publishers.
Hoffman, M. (1998) 'Time to Speak Up'. TES Primary magazine, 26 June 1998.
Jordan, R. (1998) *Meeting the Needs of Pupils with Autistic Spectrum Disorders.* Paper to NASEN Special Needs North East Conference.
Jowett, S. and Evans, C. (1996) *Speech and Language Therapy Services for Children.* Slough: National Foundation for Educational Research.
Locke, S. (1998) *Putting it into Words*: (Special, Summer 1998.) Tamworth: NASEN.
Manolson, A. (1992) *It Takes Two to Talk.* Hanen Publications: Canada (supplied in Oxon, Winslow).
McKel, D. (1990) *Not Now, Bernard.* London: Arrow (Red Fox).
National Curriculum Council (1989a) *A Framework for the Primary Curriculum,* No. 1. NCC: York.
National Curriculum Council (1989b) *Mathematics Non-Statutory Guidance.* NCC: York.
National Curriculum Council (1989c) *The National Curriculum for Pupils with Severe Learning Difficulties,* No. 9. NCC: York.
National Curriculum Council (1991, 1993) T.A.L.K, Journal of the National Oracy Project: York.
Qualifications and Curriculum Authority (1998a) *Can Do Better: Raising Boys' Achievement in English.* London: QCA.
Qualifications and Curriculum Authority (1998b) *Gathering Evidence of Children's Reading Through Talk – Key Stage 1* (video). London: QCA.
Qualifications and Curriculum Authority (1998c) *Standards at Key Stage 1, English and Mathematics: Report on the 1997 National Curriculum Assessments for 7-year-olds.* London: QCA.
Qualifications and Curriculum Authority (1998d) *Standards at Year 4, English and Mathematics: Report on the Use of Optional Tests with 9-year-olds.* London: QCA.
School Curriculum and Assessment Authority (1996) *Entering Compulsory Education* (reference to *Desirable Outcomes for Mathematics*). London: SCAA.
School Curriculum and Assessment Authority (1997) *Looking at Children's Learning.* London: SCAA.
SPACE (Science Processes and Concept Exploration) Project Research Report. Liverpool: Liverpool University Press.
Teacher Training Agency (1998) *Consultation on National Standards and Training for Specialist Teachers of Pupils with Special Educational Needs.* London: TTA.
Wagge, J. (1989) 'The role of the speech therapist', in Davies, J. D. and Davies, P. (eds) *A Teacher's Guide to Support Services.* Windsor: NFER-Nelson.
TEACCH (Treatment and Education of Autistic and Related Communication Handicapped Children) programme, in Shopler, E. and Reichler, R.J. (1983) *Individualised Assessment and Treatment for Autistic and Developmentally Disabled Children VIII – Teaching Activities for Autistic Children.* Baltimore: University Park Press.

Useful Addresses

ICT Software
Rickett Educational Media
Great Western House
Longport
Somerset
TA10 9YU

LDA (Learning Development Aids)
NES/Arnold
Ludlow Hill Road
West Bridgford
Nottingham
NG2 6HD
(re: chatter box, differentiated plays, circle time poems)

Oxford Reading Tree
Oxford University Press
Educational Supply
Saxon Way West
Corby
Northants
NN18 9BR

Performance Indicators in Primary Schools (PIPS)
Baseline Assessment
Burdon House
School of Education
University of Durham
Leazes Road
Durham
DH1 1TA

Index

ability groups 33
accents 17–18, 24
actions
  activities with 60
  as communication 3
active listening 66
adjectives 5
all-purpose vocabulary 61, **62**
analysis 64
'and', overuse of 6
appeal questions 29
application and making use of knowledge 64
art 86
Asian languages 22
assertiveness training 16
assessment and recording 25, 82–93
audience 1, 2, 23, 24, 57
audiologist 20
audit of practice 26
auditory discrimination 9, 63
autistic spectrum disorders 20, 38, 81

babies 5
bar charts 46, **47**
baseline assessment 91
behaviour plan 75
bilingual learners 22, 25, 37, 90
  see also English: as additional language
bingo 60
books for reading aloud 78
boys 42
Braille 32
Bullock Report 43, 45

calculation 50
capacity 52
case studies 53–4, 70–71, 72–3
catalogues, pictures from 79, 80
categorisation games 60–61, 80
cause and effect 52
challenging behaviour, supporting child with 75
'Chatter box' 79

child's involvement in own learning 4, 77–8, 87

circle time 65
  poems 81
class-based targets 88
class teacher 68, 72, 73, 75, 90
  see also teachers
classroom
  communication problems in 14–18
  implications of early language development for 7
  SEN specialist teachers in 71, 72, 73
  sensory impaired child in 19, 74
closed questions 28, 29
Code of Practice 69, 71, 90
  Stage 3 71, 72–3
  Stage 5 72–3
collaborative work
  with ICT 67
  see also group work
collection of items 79–80
communication
  across curriculum 35–49
  effective use of resources for 68–81
  language as 1–4
  policy for 23–6
  see also communication difficulties; communicative behaviour; language
communication difficulties 14–22, 36, 52–3, 75, 76
communicative behaviour
  development of 5–12
  as enabler or barrier 27
  focused activities for 65–7
  and policy 25
  targets for 21, 33
  see also communication
comparison 52
computer work 45, 67, 81, 86
concept
  development 76
  formation 5
conflict 42
content vocabulary 62
context
  language 62
  listening 2

continuous assessment 83, 84, 87
control questions 29
creative development 36
creative learners 56
cross-curricular work 24, 35–49
  observations 86
cumulative assessment 83, 86–7, 89

DfEE *see* Department for Education and Employment
DARTS activities 67
decimals 54
decision-making activities 38
decoding skills 31
definite article 22
Department for Education and Employment (DfEE) 7, 9, 10, 24, 75
description games and activities 60, 66, 80
design and technology 44–5
  see also technology
desirable outcomes **8**, 8–9, 35–6, 51, 91
detail
  group activity to focus on 66
  in maths 52
development of speaking and listening 5–13
diagrammatic information 46–7,
dialects 17–18, 24
dialogue in writing 92
differentiation 27, 28–30, 31, 68, 79–80
directed activities related to texts (DARTS) 67
dominant speakers 16
drama 41–3, 60, 86 *see also* plays
dressing up 60
dyslexia 18–19

early years/pre-school
  assessment 91
  development of speaking and listening 7–9
  portage 77
  talk in 35–6
educational model 74
educational psychologist 20, 68, 75
emotions 43, 81
English
  as additional language 22, 38, 90 *see also* bilingual learners
  compared with Asian languages 22
  developed through curriculum 36
  keeping records 92
  National Curriculum 4, 17
  standard 3, 4, 17, 24, 57
  talk in 41–4
equal opportunities 25
Ethnic Minority Support Services 90
evaluation
  of policy 26
  and thinking skills 64
evaluative comprehension 43
evaluative discussion 73
experiential learner 56
expressive language 6–7
  difficulties 15
external specialist teacher *see* specialist teacher

factual questions 28
familiar situations, understanding of 5
feely bag 60
filing records 87
focused language activities 55–67
  resources for 80–81
fractions 52, 53, **54**
Framework for the Primary Curriculum, A (NCC) 8
friendship groups 33
function words 62
functions of language 2–3, 6

GEP (Group Education Plan) 66, 83
games 38, 59–61, 65–6, 80
gender 24 *see also* boys
geography 36, 86
gesture 2, 64
goals 4
  joint 33
  see also targets
governors 68
grammar 6, 7, 9, 31–2
graphs **46**, 46
Group Education Plan (GEP) 66, 83
group work 16, 24, 32–3, 40, 50, 51, 80, 84, 85, 86
  games and activities 65–6, 80–81
guided reading and writing 33

happy families 61
head teacher 68
health and safety 44
hearing aids 19
hearing impaired children 19, 32, 74
history 36, 86
home visits 77
homonyms 30
human resources 68–78

I spy 60
IEP *see* Individual Education Plan
improvised drama 42
incoherent speakers 16–17
independence 22, 25, 33–4
independent activities 84
Individual Education Plan (IEP) 4, 14, 21–2, 28, 29, 33, 57, 61, 69, 71, 76, 77-8, 83,88, 89, 90
Information and Communication Technology (ICT) 45, 67, 81
information to knowledge 35, 45–9
initial communication 5–7
instructions 39–40, 44, 52, 61, 63, 66
interpretation 64
interviews 66

joint goals 33, **33**

Key Stage 1 9–11, 17, 31, 35, 36–7, 41, 73, 79, 92
Key Stage 2 11, 37, 41, 42, 79, 81, 92
Key Stage 3 11, 81, 92
Key Stage 4 11
Kim's game 60
knowledge, turning information into 35, 45–9

LEA *see* local education authority
LSA *see* learning support assistant
language
  areas 12–13, 24–5
  as communication 1–4
  context 62, **62**
  development 5
  development targets 21
  effective use of resources for 78–81
  elements 13
  focused activities 55–67
  and learning styles 56–7
  mathematical 51–2
  and poetry and literature 43–4
  policy for 23–6
  skills 3, 27
  strategies 3
  see also communication; language difficulties; language unit
language difficulties 14–22, 36, 52–3, 75, 76
language disorders 19–20, 29
language unit 20
learning
  child's involvement in 4, 77–8, 87
  styles 56–7
learning difficulties 36, 64–5 *see also* communication difficulties; moderate learning difficulties; SEN; severe learning difficulties
learning support assistant (LSA)
  and assessment 83, 85, 88–9, 90
  brief mentions 18, 22, 45
  as human resource 69–71
  and material resources 79, 80
  and policy 25
  training 71, 74, 75
length 52
letters 79
listening
  active 66
  assessing and recording 82–93
  contexts 2
  developing listening skills 63
  development 5–13
  effective use of resources for 68–81
  focused activities for 55–67
  interrelationship of language skills 4
  National Curriculum 4
  policy for 23–6
  poor 15
  see also specialised language and communication difficulties; talk
literacy 4, 48, 61, 81
literacy coordinator 25, 68
literacy hour
  brief mentions 41, 69, 73
  cross-curricular work in 48
  DARTS activities in 67
  and hearing impaired child 19
  and semantic–pragmatic language disorders 20
  talk in 27–34, 78, 83–5
literature 43
local education authority (LEA) 20, 22, 42, 69, 74
  Educational Development Plan 72
  portage service 77
  Special Educational Needs Support Service 71
Looking at Children's Learning (SCAA) 8

mainstream schools 19, 75 *see also* primary schools; secondary schools
material resources 25, 78–81
maths 49, 50–54, 61, 85, **86**, 92
maths trail 52
measuring 50
medical model 74
medical officer 20
metaphors 43–4
moderate learning difficulties 38, 75
money 52

mother tongue assessment 90
multi-disciplinary team 20
multi-sensory approaches 23, 61
multiplication 54

NHS trusts 74
NLS *see* National Literacy Strategy
NNS *see* National Numeracy Strategy
naming
  focus on 39
  games and activities 60, 80
National Curriculum
  and assessment 82
  and cross-curricular work 35, 36–7, 48
  and desirable outcomes 8, 91
  English 4, 17
  Level 1 10
  Level 2 9, 10, **11**
  Level 3 11, **12**
  Level 4 11, **12**
  maths 50, 53
  and policy 24
  working towards 7
national feedback 92
National Literacy Strategy (NLS)
  brief mentions 68, 73
  and cross-curricular work 4, 35, 37, 41, 42, 48
  and literacy hour 27, 30, 31, 33, 67
  objectives 9, 10–11, 83
  and policy 24
  and standard English 17
  word lists 62, 84
National Numeracy Strategy (NNS) 24, 35, 49, 50, 51, 54, 68, 69
National Oracy Project 55, 57, 65
nouns 5
Nuffield Foundation 47
number 50, 51
  lines 46
numeracy coordinator 68
numeracy hour 50–54, 69, 78, 85
Numeracy in Action (BBC TV) 51
Numeracy Matters (DfEE) 50

objects 60, 79
observation 73, 83, 86, 88, 89
observation questions 28
open questions 28–30
opinions 66
opportunities for speaking and listening 4, 24–5
'opposites' cards 79

PE (physical education) 44, 53
PIPS (Performance Indicators in Primary Schools) 91
pair work 84
parents 24, 25–6, 36, 68, 75–7, 89–90
Performance Indicators in Primary Schools (PIPS) 91
permanence, awareness of 5
persuasive speaking 5
philosophy 23
phonics 31
phonological awareness 9, 31
photographs 79
phrases 6
physical education (PE) 44, 53
pictures 32, 40, 43, 58, 60, 61, 79, 80
pie charts **46**
planning language activities 61–3
play 76 *see also* games
plays 79 *see also* drama
plenary
  literacy hour 34
  numeracy hour 51
Plowden Report 4
plurals 22
poetry 43–4
  circle time poems 81
policy for language and communication 23–6
portage 77
postcards 79
practical subjects, communication through 44–5
pragmatic disorder *see* semantic–pragmatic language disorders
precise learners 56
prepositions 5, 22, 44, 83
pre-school children see early years/pre-school
primary schools 50
principles, policy 23–4
problem solving
  general 38
  mathematical 53
procedures 24–6
pronouns 22
Punjabi 22
purchased equipment 79
purpose 2, 23, 24, 57

Qualifications and Curriculum Authority (QCA) 7, 9, 10, 42, 84, 92
question games and activities 59–60, 61
questions
  appeal 29
  and assessment 83, **84**
  and bilingual learners 22

child who rarely asks 17
closed 28, 29
control 29
differentiated 28–30
encouraging 17, 66
factual 28
focusing on question words 58–9
and maths 51, 52
observation 28
open 28–30
purpose of 29–30
reasoning 28
social 29
see also question games and activities

reading 4, 9, 23, 27, 28, 31, 33, 36, 37, 48, 67
assessment 84, 88
books to read aloud 78
conference 86–7
reasoning questions 28
Reception year, assessment in 91
receptive language 5–6
Record of Achievement 87
repetition 78
resources 25, 68–81
role-play 16, 41, 57–8
roles and responsibilities 25, 68–9, 74

SCAA 91
SEN 4, 20, 21, 22, 25, 27, 28, 67, 68, 69, 71, 72, 73, 75, 76, 77, 81, 83
see also Individual Education Plan; specialised language and communication difficulties; specialist teacher
SEN specialisms, training in 75
SEN specialist teacher *see* specialist teacher
SENCO (special educational needs coordinator) 25, 68, 70, 71, 72, 74, 90
SLD *see* severe learning difficulties
SPACE project 47–8
schools
listening contexts in 2
mainstream provision for SEN 75
primary 50
range of adults available 68
secondary 11–12, 37–8
speaking functions in 2–3
and support for SEN 71–2
see also classroom
science 39, 47–8, 92
secondary school 11–12, 37–8
semantic–pragmatic language disorders 19–20, 29
sensory impaired children 32, 74 *see also* hearing impaired children
sentence chain 61
sentences
focused word and sentence work 30–32
games 61
and language development 6
and poetry 43
and QCA report 92
sequence 52
sequential learners 56
severe learning difficulties (SLD) 20–21, 32, 38, 45, 53, 64
shapes 52
shared work 28, 83, 84
shy children 16
silly sentences 61
'Simon says' activities 63
social questions 29
social referencing 64
social situations/contexts 41, 57–8
sorting games 60
sounds *see* auditory discrimination
speaking
assessing and recording 82–93
developing speaking skills 63–4
development 5–13
effective use of resources for 68–81
expressive language difficulties 15
focused activities for 55–67
interrelationship of language skills 4
National Curriculum 4
policy for 23–6
problems in classroom 16–18
range of functions in school 2–3
see also specialised language and communication difficulties; talk
special educational needs *see* SEN
special educational needs coordinator *see* SENCO
specialised language and communication difficulties 18–21
specialist teacher 25, 69, 71–3, 75, 90
specialists *see* support; name of specialist/speciality
speech and language therapy 20, 69, 70, 73–4, 76
spelling 31
staff development 24, 25 *see also* training
standard English 3, 4, 17, 24, 57
statements
of information 52
true or false 61

stories 43, 58, 63
subject dictionaries 40, **41**
subject vocabulary 37, 38–41, 62, 77
summative assessment 83
support 25, 36, 68–75, 90
symbolic understanding 5
synthesising 64

TEACCH 81
talk
  assessing and recording 82–93
  central role of 94
  cross-curricular 35–8
  and DARTS 67
  and diagrammatic information 46
  in English 41–4
  in literacy hour 27–34, 78
  in numeracy hour 50–54, 78
  and parents 76, 77
  talking about 55–6
  see also listening; speaking
targets 21–2, 33, 34, 69, 70, 71, 83, 88, 89, 90
Teacher Training Agency 71, 75
teachers
  as assessors 83, 84, 88, 92
  see also class teacher; specialist teacher
technology 86 *see also* design and technology
tenses 6
thinking 1, 53, 54, 64 *see also* thought processes
thought processes 58, 59, 64 *see also* thinking
time
  lines 46
  and maths 51
  for talk 78
topic work 55–6
toys, concept development through 76
training
  courses 74
  LSAs 71, 74
  parents and voluntary helpers 76
  on resources 79
  responsibilities 68
  in SEN specialisms 75
  see also assertiveness training; staff development
true or false game 61
turn-taking games 66

understanding
  growth of 5–6
  problems with 14–15
Urdu 22

Venn diagrams 46
verbal dyspraxia 18
verbs 5, 44 *see also* tenses
visual discrimination skills 9
visual skills 2 *see also* visual discrimination skills
visually impaired children 32, 74
vocabulary *see* words/vocabulary
voluntary helpers 68, 69, 76–7, 79
  see also parents

'washing line' sequence 79–80
weight 52
whole-class work
  and assessment 83
  in numeracy hour 50, 51
  talk 28–32
word order 22
words/vocabulary
  all-purpose 61
  and children with SLD 64
  content 62
  in context 62
  focused work on 30–32, 58–9, 61–2, **62**, 83, **84**
  function 62
  and language development 5, 6, 9, 11, 30
  and NLS 9, 11, 30, 84
  question 58–9
  software programs 81
  subject 37, 38–41, 62, 77
  see also word order
workshops, parental 77
writing 4, 9, 23, 27, 28, 33, 36, 37, 48, 84, 88, 92
  conference 86–7